RESCUING OUR SONS

8 Solutions to Our Crisis of Disaffected Teen Boys

DR. JOHN DUFFY

Bestselling author of *Parenting the New Teen in the Age of Anxiety* and *The Available Parent*

mango
PUBLISHING
CORAL GABLES

For permission requests, please contact the publisher at:

Mango Publishing Group

2850 S Douglas Road, 2nd Floor

Coral Gables, FL 33134 USA

info@mango.bz

For special orders, quantity sales, course adoptions and corporate sales, please email the publisher at sales@mango.bz. For trade and wholesale sales, please contact Ingram Publisher Services at customer.service@ingramcontent.com or +1.800.509.4887.

Rescuing Our Sons: 8 Solutions to Our Crisis of Disaffected Teen Boys

Library of Congress Cataloging-in-Publication number: 2023936075

ISBN: (pb) 978-1-68481-368-1 (hc) 978-1-68481-369-8 (e) 978-1-68481-370-4

BISAC category code FAM043000, FAMILY & RELATIONSHIPS / Life Stages / Teenagers

RESCUING
OUR
SONS

To Walt, Georgiana, and all the boys
I've had the honor to work with

Table of Contents

Part One

An Emerging Realization

Any day can be trying for a therapist. You just never know what emotional issues will arrive in the room at any time. At ten, I may be helping a family work through a loss, or personality clashes. By noon, I may be helping a teenager gain some perspective over a breakup or an unexpectedly bad grade. After work, a young adult may be managing profound depression or anxiety.

I've been doing this gig for a while, and I've noticed that as the years pass, the possibility of deep emotional difficulty showing up unannounced in any given hour is increasingly likely.

But I started to notice another shift a couple of years ago. Typically, on any given day, my after-school therapy schedule is split between boys and girls and young men and young women. My work week would take on a fairly predictable cadence, or at least as predictable as can be expected for a therapist.

My Tuesdays, however, were starting to wipe me out. I would come home exhausted and spent, feeling as if I'd emotionally and intellectually left all I had on the proverbial playing field of the therapy room. Within an hour of arriving home, I'd often drop into bed, depleted. My Wednesdays, on the other hand, would find me leaving the office with energy, hope, and a literal spring in my step. No doubt, I was happier leaving the office on Wednesday nights than I was on Tuesdays.

I was really beginning to wonder what was going on. What was the big difference between Tuesdays and Wednesdays? I saw about the same number of clients. Ages didn't seem to drive the difference. And there was nothing demonstrably distinct going on in my life to suggest I would feel so differently over the course of twenty-four short hours, week after week.

I'm a pretty high-energy guy, and I found that the most obvious 'tell' regarding the difference between the days was, of all things, my coffee. Each morning, I'd stop at the Starbucks around the corner and pick up a venti iced coffee, black. In my mind, that large cup of super-charged caffeine ensured that I would make it through the day as attentive and upbeat with my last client as I was with my first, and as wide awake at ten at night as I was at nine in the morning.

But as I began to pay attention to this Tuesday vs. Wednesday thing, I noticed a recurrent change in my coffee consumption. On Tuesdays, that giant cup of Starbucks would be drained every week. I needed every drop to hang in with my clients and to really give their therapy my all. On Wednesdays, I had the venti at the ready if called upon, but I rarely drank much of it. In fact, I found myself pouring out half or more of the cup at the end of the day. A day with the same number of therapy hours as the day before. With people of about the same age.

But I was working harder on Tuesdays.

As nothing like this had ever happened before in my twenty-five-year career, I thought I'd launch a little investigation and look into this bizarre phenomenon. It didn't take long.

I opened the calendar on my iPhone and scanned my recent weeks. The answer jumped off the screen.

On Tuesdays, my clients were boys and young men. On Wednesdays, they were girls and young women. That was it, the singular difference between the two days of the week.

I sat there a bit dumbfounded and considered this reality for a while. The more I thought about it, the less sense it made to me. Regardless of gender, my clients—boys and girls, men and women—came to therapy for similar reasons. They were anxious about their futures as well as their present. They were depressed about their lives, and low self-worth and a poor sense of self-image permeated both genders. Body image and eating issues were prevalent among most of the young people I was seeing as well. The way they were seen by peers on social media was also a major stressor for both genders, with anxieties about the number of "likes" and "follows" and self-comparisons to others who seemed to have perfect lives. Concerns about the world around them, including a degree of hopelessness about a bright future for themselves and their families, were also common.

They had all also been navigating a years-long pandemic while grieving the loss of so many expected life markers—plays and proms, graduations and games, wins and losses, relationships and breakups, and smiles and tears. And they mourned the absence of just being able to have normal moments sitting with friends instead of isolating at home for months on end, unsure of what the future would look like or whether anything would ever feel normal again.

But these concerns didn't separate girls from boys or men from women. Quite the contrary, such experiences made them more similar to one another. Given the above set of mutual concerns, one might think, as I did, that I would experience no significant difference between Tuesdays, Wednesdays, or any other days of the week.

Given the deep and serious nature of these struggles, one might also wonder why I didn't drain that venti coffee every single day.

My Weekly Session Day with Girls

Teenage girls and young women are, on the whole, fascinating therapy clients. They are virtually never late. They rarely cancel scheduled appointments. Many of them bound into the room energetically. It is clear this is an hour they plan, look forward to, work for, and relish. Many of them ask me about my week and how my day is going. They don't just ask in passing—they want to know. They check in with me and make sure I'm okay. From the moment they enter the room, girls and young women are present and ready to go. They come in with energy, with *juice!*

Make no mistake. Teenage girls and young women suffer and struggle mentally and emotionally every bit as much as boys and young men. The times we're living in provide singular difficulties for our girls, without a doubt. They feel pressure to perform exceptionally well in school and to get involved in as many extracurricular activities as are reasonable, sometimes to a degree well beyond the reasonable. Perfectionism, body image issues, and negative comparisons to the lives of other girls are all trials for almost any young woman or girl today, and each of these is becoming more difficult for them as well. Online hate, the threat of sexual violence, and virtually impossible beauty standards are prominent in their minds. Too often, girls internalize these massive stressors, driving a substantial recent uptick in self-harm, self-loathing, suicidal ideation, and even completed suicides. I've read countless stories over the past year about the crisis in American girlhood and find myself nodding along as I read. Yes, our girls and young women are suffering mightily, without a doubt.

On top of all that, I've found that the girls and young women I work with *feel* a lot. They carry deep wells of empathy that often leave them serving as de facto therapists to their friends on top of everything else, supporting them wholeheartedly and guiding them through their latest social, emotional, and/or academic crises. And for many girls, the office is always open. They are available to one another at the lunch table, during class, after school, even in the middle of the night. I cannot tell you how many times a teenage girl has described a makeshift therapy session with a friend over Snapchat in total silence at two in the morning.

This phenomenon, by the way, is not without its perils. Oftentimes, kids just need an ear, and their friends, most often their female friends, are more than happy to serve that purpose. But sometimes, the issue at hand is well beyond the expertise of a fourteen-, seventeen-, or twenty-two-year-old. Sometimes kids are in danger of harming themselves or overtly suicidal when consulting with buddies. This is dangerous for both kids involved. For the sufferer, their life may actually be at risk. And for the "therapist," deep fear and guilt can often result. Better this work be left to qualified therapists.

But in reality, too often, it is not.

In any event, girls manage their therapy sessions energetically. They tell animated stories to illustrate their emotions. They share with gusto, bringing diaries and music by Taylor Swift and Olivia Rodrigo into session to provide color and illustration to my understanding of their emotional lives, and they are concerned about running out of time before they run the full intended emotional course. Like many others, one fifteen-year-old girl I work with impressively drives the content of the session, deftly switching between humor and emotion, making the hour a well-produced drama.

In any event, that's a snapshot of my typical Wednesday.

My Weekly Session Day with Boys

My sessions after school on Tuesdays stand in stark contrast to my Wednesday schedule. As I've stated, I happen to see boys and young men on Tuesdays, and they present in the therapy room in a very different way than their female counterparts.

For starters, boys often come in with far less clarity about why they're in the room. They are often listless, with little direction or energy for the work of therapy. They typically know something doesn't feel quite right in their lives and in their worlds, but often have significant difficulty articulating the nature of that phenomenon. They frequently know, for instance, that they are checked out at school or have few or no friends. They may be vaguely aware that they are not happy. But far too often, they lack the emotional language to arrive with a clear vision of the problem. So, therapy with boys and young men often starts from an entirely different point than it does with girls and young women.

We therapists often call this initial presentation in the room *resistance*: a disengagement in the process, an effort not to participate. But for our boys and young men, the concept of resistance really doesn't capture why they so often struggle in the room. Our boys are working through a couple of significant obstacles specific to them. First, we have to remember that we still fail to raise our boys with a wealth of emotional language. They therefore understand their own emotions and emotional life, as well as those of others, far less readily than girls. They feel good or bad, fine or lousy. The words available to us matter, and on the whole, boys are working with a depleted emotional vocabulary, a topic which I will expand on later.

Boys also lack a certain familiarity with intimate contact and discussion, hallmarks of connected and effective therapy. Whereas girls fully engage with me on Wednesdays, boys struggle to look me in the eye on Tuesdays. Boys often grapple with putting down their phones and engaging, and this often comes across to me as a need to be distracted in order to interact. I noticed that one boy in his late teens could only talk about his emotions while looking at his phone.

Eye contact was too much for him emotionally, and he feared he might cry, the idea of which was a horror to him. I've noticed that girls, on the other hand, put their phones away at the onset of a session, or they make sure I know they are turning it off. I take this as notification of their readiness to engage and as a call for me to be prepared to fully engage as well.

This is part of what makes Tuesdays so difficult. The stream of progress flows far less quickly for boys because we have a different starting point altogether, a shallow well of emotional language and ability to connect from which to draw.

Boys also don't have a solid bead on their place in the therapy room. They experience conflicting emotions about the very fact of being here, with a therapist, to talk about themselves and their emotional lives. They experience a vague sense of shame that they might *need* to be here, that they cannot suck it up, *man up*, and manage these things on their own. On a subconscious level, we continue to deliver this sense of independence and stoicism as core to what it means to be a boy, a man, to be *masculine*. So, just to begin the work of therapy, we have to manage the dissonance of masculinity.

Finally, and importantly, boys and young men are also telling me that they are hearing a couple of clear messages from the culture at large. The first is that this is not their time. The idea here is that men have held nearly the entirety of the cultural focus forever, and it is now time for girls and women to shine. And honestly, most of the young guys I work with understand this notion, and by and large, they support this idea. But along with that support for their female counterparts, boys are understandably confused about what their role now ought to be. Do they remain on the sidelines? Do they march in support? Should they just shut up?

These questions lead to another point of disparate feelings for our boys. Not only do they feel this is not their time, but many of them have told me they feel as if they have been the cause of the problems that plague our society, that they have victimized both the girls and young women they know and those they may not know at all. Boys come into the room feeling as if they themselves *are* the problem.

And it is working through all this muck with boys and young men that sucks the air out of my Wednesdays. I need every drop of caffeine to help guide these boys through the slog of low emotional IQs, as well as hopelessness and confusion about their identities and where they belong in the world.

I suspect that since you've picked up this particular book, you are not only concerned with the state of affairs for our boys in general, but are experiencing some unease about your boy, or your boys and young men, in particular. You are already likely aware that our boys are going through a difficult time and that their well-being is at risk in so many ways. So, with each issue I present here, I will include some expert tips for helping your boys navigate and manage some of the difficult times and issues they may be experiencing.

Boys in Crisis

Our boys and young men are in crisis. Doing what I do for a living, sitting across from these young boys and watching the life force slowly drain out of them, I feel a responsibility to share what I know and what I see. I suspect there are very few of us, with most of those in my field, who understand the depth, breadth, and degree of the crisis boys are going through. They need our help in discovering who they are and how they fit in this world. They need our gentleness amidst the harshness that makes up so much of their lives. They need our absolute and unconditional positive regard so that they can see the beauty and character and strength they carry within them. In effect, they need us to lead a paradigm shift in the way we look at them, and certainly in the way they look at themselves.

More and more, I see self-loathing in young men and boys. There are a couple of factors involved here. First, we don't always give them very good feedback about who they are. Boy behavior isn't always endearing. Boys can be messy. Teenage boys can be particularly difficult; they can be so disagreeable. They can eat awful food, vape nicotine or marijuana day and night, play horrific video games until all hours, stare at their phones, disappear into their rooms, phone in their schoolwork, and shut down when we try and talk to them.

Teenage boys can be a pain in the ass.

And they can seem all but impossible to parent effectively, especially in comparison to their female counterparts. So as parents, we don't always bring our best to teenage boys, in part because they don't always bring their best to us. So, we know that we can be short tempered with them. If they're argumentative, we have a tendency to be argumentative back. Their silence when asked to do something or merely to answer a simple question can be maddening. So they see our angriest selves. I get it.

Teenage boys can be a huge pain in the ass.

But I want you to know that our boys are in a very rough spot emotionally right now. Emotionally, I feel the boys I work with deteriorating. The light in the eyes of a lot of these boys is fading fast. And I have the luxury of knowing these boys in a therapy setting: In this room, they are not a pain in the ass. They are so sweet, so kind, so very funny, and so thoughtful. There are so many things that they never show you, or rarely do.

But teenage boys today find themselves in this logistical jam that many of them can't think their way out of. Most of their lives now, they've heard that they are a problem. They are the bad guys or, if they're not yet, they're going to be. Because that's what men do. They are the harsh players in our society. They're emotionally removed and unavailable. They can have a propensity for violence if they are not attended to as expected by women. And they're the ones most likely to say the terrible racist or misogynistic things—the things that get people canceled. And maybe they deserve it, they think.

But they also know that they're not these people. They love and respect the girls around them and their sisters and their mothers. They rarely if ever think a racist thought, though they're pretty sure their fathers did, and their fathers' fathers before them. Many of them feel like they're paying the price for sins committed generations ago having nothing at all to do with them.

So, a couple of things happen. Some of these boys become angry and resentful. They listen to the most vitriolic podcasts and watch the most hateful television shows. They adopt a mindset of scarcity, that something has been taken away from them, some birthright by virtue of the fact that they are male. There are powerful pitchmen selling these ideas to our boys in the quiet of their bedrooms, through earbuds so that we can't hear a word of it. Recruitment is unfortunately going very well.

Many other boys approach this very differently. They retreat into themselves, unsure what to do or fundamentally who they are. This is not an identity crisis, it's a total lack of identity. With no clear idea of who they are, who they should be, or who they want to be, these boys become anxious and depressed. Many of them smoke weed or play video games or stare at other screens nearly constantly in a disappearing act, not quite suicidal, but not at all alive either.

I'm worried about the emotional well-being of all of these boys. Their gentle nature is either sharpened to a very fine and angry point or blunted until it is entirely dull and lifeless. Some of you who have picked up this book are nodding along here, I know. You see your sons in the paragraphs above. Your heart is broken because even though you can recognize what he's up against, you're not at all sure how to guide him through it. After all, these are not the same challenges their fathers went through or their fathers before them. These are new challenges.

They require a new type of parenting. To help our boys address all of this, we need to be the greatest communicators parents have ever been. We have to have the patience to draw our boys out. We effectively need to become therapists in our home, accepting that it's going to take time for them to come around. They are going to be a pain in the ass for quite some time before they figure out who they are. And at least part of that is going to happen through our eyes.

For without our patience and our unconditional positive regard for them, we know that the odds of them getting through this with their spirits intact drop precipitously. And you also probably know how mighty an ask this is. Because what their behavior often elicits from you is your ire, your disdain, your very worst. Yet we all know this is the last thing they need. They already have plenty of disdain for themselves without us doubling down on them.

This phenomenon can be terribly frustrating for parents. After all, you're good at this. You obviously read parenting books, and you pay attention. So, you must wonder, why is this not easier with your son?

I get it.

But the truth is it's not easier with him because it's not easier for him. He is struggling. All that behavior, misbehavior, or lack of behavior is symptomatic of that struggle. And deep down, you know he's not happy. You know he's conflicted and unsure. You know that, at least to some extent, his sense of self is a bit shattered, and to recognize that out loud is straight-up scary. I've been through it with parents. It sucks, no doubt.

So, I know you picked up this book with some thoughts in your mind about things you want to see change. We are going to address all of those. But as we begin, I want to make sure that you soften. Put yourself in his shoes for a moment. Empathize with his struggle and his pain. Our sweet boys are struggling. They need you to hold some of the pain associated with that struggle. They need to know that you are available to talk about it, even if they never once take you up on it, ever. Just the fact that you're there and open matters. And your fear, judgment, and ego are not the primary point—his well-being is. If you approach him with that kind of openness, love, and gentleness, the right things are going to happen whether you read another page of this book or not.

For you parents of boys, I want you to know that I feel for you. I know this is hard. I've been through this struggle with so many parents now over the last few years. And as you read on here, you'll find out that I too am going to be a bit of a pain in the ass.

I'm going to be pesky, repetitive, and redundant. I will be saying the same thing over and over. I will be encouraging you to listen more than you talk over and over again. Because it's so hard to get these things the first time through. I'm the therapist in the situation, and I find it hard myself sometimes. I get frustrated. I mess it up frequently.

I don't expect you to be perfect, not at all. If your guy knows you're available to him, that's all that really matters.

Stressors in Common

Across the genders, adolescence today carries a significant amount of stress, and it looks and feels different than it did a generation ago. As parents, we have to listen more than we talk. We are not the experts at being teenagers and young adults now. They are.

So, what exactly is this new set of stressors? Well, let's start with academic related stress. Kids put more academic pressure on themselves now than they ever have. They would also argue that their parents put more academic pressure on them than those parents ever experienced themselves. As a result, our young people tend to fall into one of two camps academically: They are either Type A perfectionists, or they get so overstressed they throw in the towel on academics altogether. I suspect you see your child in one of these two camps. Neither is ideal, of course. And both are attempts to manage anxiety around what feel to them like untenable or unachievable academic challenges.

I work with Aiden, a fifteen-year-old high school sophomore who has been anxiously looking forward to college admissions since middle school. He is doing his level best to take every AP class his high school offers. He is in my opinion involved in far too many extracurricular activities; he is an athlete, an actor, and a debater. Yet he is certain that is not enough.

On the other hand, I currently work with a number of high school and college age students who do literally no work whatsoever outside of class. And many of them skip classes altogether. They can see that profound academic stress their peers are suffering, so they tap out of it altogether.

We also have to keep in mind that this generation of kids just went through a pandemic. Whereas most of us grew up with some degree of certainty about the world, some elements of life we could simply rely on, this generation does not have that luxury. Many of the teenagers I work with fear there will be another pandemic or something else that will shut down their schools. So, their futures feel tenuous and uncertain to them. I don't think many of us felt that way.

Anxiety about school shootings lingers in the back of the minds of most of the young people I work with as well. In fact, many of the kids I work with have become makeshift profilers, looking sideways at male classmates, wondering if this or that one might be the next school shooter. Just imagine going through your days wondering whether violence is going to rip through your school. It's harrowing, and I find that there is not much consolation that we can provide to kids to mitigate their fears.

Though they can't imagine a world without it, social media also drives a lot of stress in young people. Whereas we grown folks had some time to be off the clock and not in view of others when we were younger, our kids don't have that space. They have to be "on" far more often since social media demands that they present a certain way to their peers. They have to manage online personas as well as the facets they bring to various other areas of their lives, including in-person interactions with their friends, family members, teachers, coaches, and all of the other people in their lives. That's a lot of others' impressions to try to manage. Add to that the threats of online bullying and cancel culture that can break a reputation with one post, and you're dealing with a significant amount of stress.

And finally, our teenagers and young adults are far more aware of their emotional well-being, or lack thereof, than we were. A generation ago, we did not talk much about depression, anxiety, attention deficit problems, or suicidal ideation. Now, these are part of a normal teenager's vernacular. It's not all bad news. Kids often support each other through their emotional difficulties on Snapchat, Instagram, or newer platforms. They are available as de facto therapists to one another virtually all the time, twenty-four hours a day.

But there's a great deal of stress associated with this as well. Teenagers should not and cannot be responsible for each other's well-being. And because there is so much talk of emotional difficulties, a lot of kids identify, and often overidentify, with one diagnosis or another. So, by the time they get into my office, some kids will tell me they are already anxious or depressed. They've looked at the diagnostic criteria; they have evaluated themselves. As a result, they often feel a sense of weakness in their own character, a defect in their fundamental makeup, a fragility in their persona. And once they have self-diagnosed, I find it very difficult to convince a teenager, male or female, that they are actually okay, that a degree of depression or anxiety is manageable. Far more often, they feel just the opposite.

To help mitigate these stressors, I strongly urge you to read on. The thoughts and tips I offer often apply not only to boys, but to any of your kids. Hang in with me here, and we will find solutions for these vexing and troubling problems and hope in situations that seem to be hopeless.

Part Two

The Boy Problem Described

Why Boys? Why Now?

Almost every problem we suffer as a society can be traced back to the suffering of boys and young men. I know that's a broad, sweeping statement, but think about it for a moment. We have been led to every war in the history of mankind at the hands of men. The vast majority of corruption in corporate America has been committed by men. Our political and news landscapes are poisoned with vitriol, the vast majority of it coming from the mouths of men. Nearly every known terrorist has been male. The vast majority of sexual assault is committed by men. Most every person attacking the US Capitol on January 6 was a man. Almost every single public mass shooting and school shooting since Columbine has been committed by a man, or a boy.

It's important that we note, uncomfortable as it may be, that these realities are not happenstance or coincidence. There are reasons that men are at the center of these cultural ills. In many ways, our boys and young men are broken. They lack the clarity they need, emotionally and otherwise, to be their best selves, quite literally. And we all pay the price for that.

Sometimes, hurting boys and men turn their self-loathing, hopelessness, loneliness, and lack of a sense of belonging inward. Sure, hurt people hurt people, but far more often, boys and young men cause harm to themselves, sometimes overtly, and at other times quite covertly. I would argue that this is why the rate of attempted and completed suicide continues to climb for boys and men, eclipsing that of girls and women by a significant margin.

But they also turn this angst outward toward the world. Lacking the full vocabulary and set of tools to find the help to heal and become emotionally healthy, they turn outward with the limited tools they have. The result of their anger and hurt may make headlines, or it may seethe quietly, almost certainly going on to infect another generation.

It is crucial to note here that men and boys are not inherently toxic. Too often, however, they lack the tools to curb toxic thoughts and behavior that can impact their minds, their families, and, in some cases, all of us in an immeasurably negative manner.

And I am well aware that boys and men have been favored by society up to the present day. Surely we have. Glass ceilings are real, and women continue to fight an uphill battle for recognition in the workplace and appreciation in the home. The pay differential between men and women remains an absurd and ongoing miscarriage of justice. The #MeToo movement is beginning to shed light on and hopefully correct decades, perhaps centuries, of the abuse of women at the hands of men. Though more households than ever before have dual incomes, women continue to do far, far more of the work of the household than men. This was true when I wrote my doctoral dissertation on this topic a quarter of a century ago, and the needle has barely moved since.

So, I want to be clear. The fight for equality and safety for women in our society as well as for people of color, for the LGBTQIA+ community, and for any underprivileged and underserved minority group, is essential. Our humanity depends on it.

And the reality is that none of these issues will be resolved as long as too many of our boys and men are broken emotionally. These issues are all complex and intertwined, and I won't purport to have all the answers to every difficulty facing society. But I can say that in my own experience, sitting across from them day after day and year after year, healing our boys and young men is a start. It has never been more crucial, and their need has never been so tremendous, as they are right now.

So, let's get into the specific issues boys and young men are suffering and what we as parents, grandparents, aunts, uncles, teachers, coaches, bosses, therapists, and other caring adults can do to help.

The Most Common Story Never Told

I recently received an email from a mom that reflected the self-image confusion our boys suffer perfectly. It was just before the middle of her son's first semester in college, around Halloween, and as far as she knew up to that point, he was thriving: acing his classes and really connecting with his professors, pledging a fraternity, and participating in intramural lacrosse. He had made, he reported, a score of good friends already and was enjoying a rich and fulfilling social life.

And then the first letter came in from the university. Before starting school, her son had signed a form allowing his parents access to his grades. And the letter said he was failing every class and, for those classes which took attendance, there was no record of his ever having attended a single class session in person since week one of this initial quarter.

Mom was understandably confused and alarmed, and certain there must be some misunderstanding. Perhaps this email was intended for different parents of a different student. Maybe the professors had made some clerical errors. She called her son, and he assured her that she was correct and that he would clear things up with the university immediately.

No big deal.

But I knew. I knew as soon as his mom wrote that initial email to me. I'd been here before with countless dozens of other teenage boys, back on my couch by Halloween, or Thanksgiving on the long end, wondering what had happened to their promising lives and why they lacked the sense of competence and resilience they believe they inherently possessed that would make moving through college to a well-paying job and a happy family life a predetermined breeze.

Like so many of his peers, this young man lied to his parents and stalled, and in doing so, he bought himself a bit of time on campus. But on his end, he knew his tenure in college was just a matter of time that was running out. He knew. He knew he had been in hiding since landing on campus. He deliberately evaded the suspicions of professors and roommates and RAs, hiding in his room almost every hour of the day. He was baffled by his inability to convince himself to engage. First, he would miss a single class. "I'll go Thursday for sure." But he would not. And the more time that passed, the darker the shadow that overcame his psyche. His future became a vast unknown to him, and his failure, in nearly every way discernible, became all but a certainty.

So, why not sit in that room and regress to childhood, playing video games and ordering junk food? Why not smoke pot morning, noon, and night to self-medicate the growing sense of dread about the comeuppance that feels imminent, as well as the haunting depression and anxiety? To all too many of these boys, pot, gaming, and self-isolation can come to feel like a balm, blurring and easing their feelings of inferiority and uselessness—emotions that are frequently at the root of these behaviors.

In my work, this is the most common story never told. A young man appears to himself, as well as to his parents and everyone else around him, to have the tools to head off into the world successfully. But as soon as he lands in that collegiate setting, without the foundation of family and the infrastructure of a planned school day he's been relying on his entire life to that point, he disappears. He cannot cope.

It's absolutely heartbreaking.

In my experience, this phenomenon takes place solely in the case of young men. I work with twelve to fifteen freshman boys a year who get to campus and suddenly fail to thrive. In the ten or so years since I've been tracking it, I cannot recall working with one young woman presenting this way. And these freshman boys, they don't plan to fail. But a powerful sense of anxiety and strikingly poor self-esteem serve as anchors preventing them from engaging with a vast new world literally surrounding them as they isolate themselves in their dorm rooms.

And many of these boys sheepishly pack up and head home before the end of that first semester. Once home, they tend to stay in their bedrooms or basements, filled with shame for failing to make it work. They see their friends enjoying campus life in every way on social media, amplifying their sense of failure, their feelings of shame. They do little to help out around the house. They're reluctant to go out and get a job or take a class. They stay up all night watching TV or pornography or both. They tend to sleep away most of the day. They often smoke weed mornings, afternoons, and evenings. One young man told me recently, "We don't even smoke to get high. It's a disappearing act, an induced coma until life gets better, I guess."

Some of these young men have told me they considered suicide before therapy. I suspect many take their own lives before ever setting foot in a therapist's office.

This is an illustration of the plight of our boys and young men today. Far too often, the little bit of hope and self-worth they carry is more fragile than we know, and their tenuous resilience cannot stand the test that their post-childhood life provides. They disappear. They induce a coma-like state, hoping that something in their lives will magically improve.

From what I have seen, years can pass for young men in this situation.

I assure you, I'm neither exaggerating nor being alarmist. I sat down to write this book in the first place because of this oft-recurring situation. It's *alarming!* Because it feels so shameful to these young men and their families, I suspect I have either the luxury or the burden of seeing how life plays out for them. And after years of experience with them, I also know how you can either help to prevent this phenomenon in your son's life, or help him through it if he comes to this pass.

Expert Tip: What We Can and Cannot Do as Parents

Now, our inclination as parents in the wake of this failed first semester is to focus on behavior. "If he would just do X, he would feel Y, and then he'd be free of these demons." Makes sense in theory. So, as a result, young men are languishing in basements everywhere, sleeping until noon or one or two in the afternoon, reluctantly driving DoorDash deliveries or Uber for a couple of hours a day to sustain their smoking or vaping habit, then playing video games and looking at social media on their phones, ceremonially visiting their friends on faraway campuses leading ideal lives, the lives they envisioned for themselves. These activities are often punctuated by procrastination or arguing with their parents, supporting positions and behaviors even they themselves don't really believe in. It's a pointless, exhausting cycle, a nightmarish Groundhog Day spent hiding from the world—and more importantly, desperately avoiding their own deep, bitter sense of self-loathing.

Most importantly, they feel no better about themselves than they did when they were languishing on campus. Quite the contrary, they feel that their inability to manage this world, a world of regression, low risk, and total safety, punctuates their uselessness and worthlessness in this world.

These young men do not need us to go hard on them. Nobody, and I mean absolutely nobody, wants to be in the position these young men find themselves in. Nobody wants to feel about themselves the way they feel about themselves.

They do *not* need us to double down on them. They've got that part of the equation more than covered.

Despite what from the outside of their minds would appear to be a lazy, thoughtless way of life, these men are thinking constantly. Internally, they are working harder than you would ever believe to figure themselves out.

I want you to really pause here and as best you can, get your mind into the head of a young man in this position in life. Consider what you think it's like to be him. Could he possibly be happy? At this point, could he possibly carry any useful modicum of hope? If you have a young man in this situation in life, or at a similar point, find a sense of empathy for him. If you are struggling to do so, ask him how he feels, without judgment, with curiosity, with love.

You will find empathy for him pretty quickly, and that empathy will draw you toward a deeper and deeper understanding of his emotional life and the degree to which it drives what he does, and also what he does not do. Then, ask him what he needs. He may not know, but he will know he has an ally in you. I can tell you with a strong degree of certainty that he needs an ally now more than ever in his life. Your alliance with him shows him he's not alone, that you will collaborate with him in navigating this storm.

Only when that connection is firmly established can you begin to brainstorm and problem-solve with him and help him determine what to do next, even if his first step is a relatively small one. After all, we are looking for little wins here, building a sense of identity, self-worth, and self-esteem that will serve as the building blocks for his future.

Now, I'll offer a bit of my clinical opinion here. His sense that you are his ally will help, without a doubt. But once a young man is in this situation, professional help is needed. I don't believe that therapy is the answer to every little bump life hands us, but we are talking about sweeping change in the ways a young man sees himself, the world, and the future. There is a lot involved here, and true, diagnosable mental illness, as well as a potentially strong reliance on one drug or another, recreational or prescribed (or both), may likely be powerful variables in the equation. So, guide your son or the struggling young man in your life toward a qualified therapist, one who has abundant experience working with these problems, specifically in young men.

I've worked with many families who felt that the gender of the therapist is perhaps the single most important variable in therapeutic success and believed a male therapist is required to do this work. But trust me, this is not the case. The right experience and the ability to connect and understand without judgment matter far more.

Once therapy is under way and a solid connection is established, I find that change tends to come rather quickly. These men find their footing and new perspectives on themselves and their place in the world and are ready to head back to college, trade school, work, or whatever their next adventure in life might happen to be.

Finally, I should note here that the difficulty of your son or the young man in your life may look different than the college freshman I describe above. I use this example as a template for the plight of our young guys today, but there are of course variations and degrees of opting out that he may exhibit. In the end, even if your son seems to be "functioning" in life perfectly well, I strongly caution you not to assume that he is in fact perfectly fine. Some young men perfect the art of seeming okay when they are really having a hard time inside. Some may not even be aware of the degree of their suffering.

This is important. Check in with your guys frequently, and gently, kindly, ask how they are doing. Remember that the world around them, and in particular, in their own minds, feels harsh and unforgiving. Let them know that they always have a soft place to fall in you—always. Trust me, they need that. They may never tell you so or even consciously realize it, but they need that.

Emotional Language

As stated earlier, we have to teach boys to understand and recognize their emotions. Where girls typically arrive in therapy with a fairly complete and accurate assessment of their emotional lives and their triggers in their minds, homes, school, and online, boys often lack this skill set. This difference is significant. The language itself is a necessary tool for healing, yet far too often, it is still lacking in our boys.

Just in my own practice, I witness this phenomenon nearly daily. I'll ask a teenage boy or young man how he's been feeling, or how he feels about something going on in his life, and he struggles to describe it. It's often clear he is carrying a strong feeling, but words evade him. A typical exchange is a struggle. Here's an example from a recent Tuesday session:

"So, your girlfriend broke up with you. How are you feeling about that?"

"I'm pissed, you know. Everything seemed fine, and she just broke it off."

"Yeah, I get it, and I can tell you're angry. But give me an idea of what else you're going through."

"I miss her, I guess. That's about it."

"It actually sounds like more than that. You seem sad about it, even broken-hearted, and I know from the way you've talked about her that you'll probably miss her."

"Yeah, I guess."

This was a difficult exchange, not only because he was having a hard time labeling his emotions. It also felt as if he didn't feel entitled to feel the way he did, as if it would display some weakness or a lack of internal fortitude to identify and express his feelings. In fact, as this conversation continued, my client broke down in tears. I sat in silence, hoping he would experience some catharsis from an expression of emotion he really could not contain or control. Instead, he simply said, "This is embarrassing."

Embarrassing.

That about sums up the emotional experience of many young men. "I shouldn't feel this way," or more to the point, "I shouldn't feel."

An enormous problem emerges for our boys when they both lack the emotional language to properly express their feelings and feel ashamed of those feelings. When those negative emotions get bottled up and accumulate, the only acceptable method of emotional release is through anger or aggression or both. Our boys and young men fail to discover the richness and nuance of their own emotional lives, and they cannot fully understand and empathize with those of others.

Though this has been true for decades, we are at a point in our history where a sweeping cultural change is not only possible but imperative.

Expert Tip: Expand Your Emotional Language with Your Boys

Take a moment and do a quick gut check. Do you use emotional language when talking to your boys? Do you talk about how you feel in different situations, like after a conflict with a friend, a bad workday, or a personal victory? Do you ask him how he feels when he experiences a difficult situation? Or how those around him feel? I should tell you that in my experience, we tend to fail mightily in this regard without even knowing it. Though we talk a big game in our culture about raising our boys and girls more and more the same in this regard, this is decidedly not true.

So, I encourage you to gradually integrate emotional language into the repertoire of your communication with your boys, including in their presence. If you're a parent who asks, "How was your day?" which I love, try to add, "How are you feeling?" He may not be drawn to this at first, but that's okay. Be persistent. In fact, you might let him know you plan to be persistent, and why. You know that it's important for him to understand himself and his world from an emotional perspective, and you not only want him to experience the richness this will add to his life, you also want him to be able to articulate how he's feeling, both to himself and with others so that he will have emotional awareness of what's going on for him if and when he ever needs help.

I'll impart two final important notes here. First, I want you to know that once they are introduced to this language and given overt permission to use it, boys respond really, really well. They can generate a degree of emotional intelligence quickly. I don't want you going into this thinking this is a massive new element of parenting you need to integrate. On the contrary, I believe you'll find that your boys and young men will adopt this language with grace and ease. They just need an introduction to emotional language, as well as an overt invitation to express their feelings to counterbalance the lack of overall cultural support for the emotional lives of boys and young men. What I'm asking you to participate in is a sweeping cultural shift. But it costs you nothing but time and consideration. And it can, quite honestly, change and save lives.

That said, I also want to offer a word of caution. You need to be aware of the possibility that once your boy's eyes are open to this language, you may well learn that he is suffering with depression, anxiety, or other issues that until now he may not have been able to label, identify, and articulate. It's not just suggestibility you're seeing here. It's clarity.

Case Study: Me

When I was fourteen years old, I began experiencing massive panic attacks that often took me to the verge of passing out. I frequently feared I was dying, and I was certain I was the only person who ever experienced this issue. Lacking the emotional language to describe to my parents or friends what I was going through, I suffered in silence, feeling that these episodes were a singular sign of weakness. I was deeply ashamed of myself, and that feeling persisted for years.

In fact, these episodes continued well into my twenties. By then, I was experiencing at least one significant episode a day, if not more. One day, I suffered a panic attack that scared me enough to stop by an emergency room. Two minutes into an interview, the doc told me I had been experiencing panic and anxiety and provided the names of a therapist. I was so relieved that my *thing* actually had a name. Over time, I realized that many, many people suffer similarly. In fact, I've treated panic and other anxiety issues countless times over the years.

But remember, until my mid-twenties, I had no idea what I was suffering every single day. In all these years as a therapist, I'm sorry to report that many of our boys are in similar situations, lacking the emotional language to understand themselves, and errantly labeling themselves weak, or stupid, or worthless. This is painfully common. And the beginning of healing is the emotional language too many of our boys and young men lack. You truly cannot talk to your boys enough about this issue. As I experienced in my own journey, it's remarkable when a boy or young man recognizes his feelings in new language, allowing hope and relief to rapidly replace fear or self-loathing. It's no small thing.

Outside Influence: The Voices

So, with all this hopelessness and confusion our boys carry, where do they turn?

Historically, we parents have been the primary influence on our kids' thinking. That is still very much the case, even for our boys. Too often, however, I'm finding that our boys and young men are not particularly interested in what we have to say. Too often, they tell me that they hear the very worst about themselves from their parents. They hear from parents that they're not trying hard enough and that they're not behaving appropriately.

They are told that they're not good enough unless and until they change, with messages like, "Stop playing those damn video games," "Work harder in school," "Get some direction in your life," "Quit smoking pot," "Stop sneaking around," "Get up off that couch," "Do something," "Do *better.*"

Honestly, I've learned in my experience working with families that we typically come from the very best of intentions when we bring this kind of criticism. Families have often been through years of frustration, therapy, and even medication by this point. Of course, we want the very best for our boys and young men. We want them to be happy. We want them to feel strong and competent and resilient. We want them to enjoy deep, rich relationships.

So when they resist our efforts to create space for all of that in their lives, we become frustrated and angry with them. Because instead of connecting, they too often disappear. Instead of putting in the work, they tap out. Instead of thriving, they flounder. Your efforts and disappointment clash with his negative feelings and sense of hopelessness about himself and his life.

And at some point, because it is critical, because it is predictable, because your perceived, profound disappointment is too much to bear, your voice drifts away. And your son—even though I know you love him with all your heart and you see the potential of the entire world in him—feels alone, adrift.

And then he hears a voice from the abyss that resonates, from a podcast, TV show, YouTube video, or an ad in the middle of a video game. It's a powerful voice, a voice that makes sense, that allows your son freedom to grab the reins and take what's his in this world. The voice carries promise that his future is bright and his fears are lies. I've seen hopeless, deeply depressed boys and young men after discovering this voice, and their sudden clarity is striking. It's downright inspired.

But there's a problem.

See, the Voices are empowering, but not really. They're vaguely inspiring, but the Voices carry an agenda of their own. The Voices have paid very close attention to our boys, and those Voices are capitalizing on the needs of our boys.

The voice is recruiting. Whether intentional or not, the voice is recruiting our boys into believing something has been taken from them, some birthright has been denied them, the world is treating them unfairly, and that's why they feel what they feel.

You may wonder why we're spending so much time on these Voices. It is because they are silently shaping the points of view of our boys and young men. And because they are so discreet, delivered on a screen or through earbuds, we may not be aware of them at all. I can feel a shift in a boy's point of view between sessions, just a week apart. To be clear, I am not bringing this issue up because of any particular political point of view. I simply want you to be aware that there are voices other than your own that could be making an enormous impact on your son's identity.

Because they are just figuring out who they are in adolescence, teenage boys are particularly susceptible to these voices. It is therefore crucial that we are not only aware of the voices they are hearing, but that our voices are in the mix as well. I therefore encourage you to sit down and watch what your son is watching and listen to what he's listening to. The Voices are slick and cunning, and they can come in the form of a

TV show, YouTube videos, Snapchat stories, or podcasts. As all of us do, boys tend to confirm their biases with the content they consume.

Too often, I find their young minds often close prematurely, precluding them from considering other points of view. In the end, this can be dangerous for them because many of the Voices that are trying to gain the attention of our sons can at times be angry and destructive. They can urge our boys to believe they are being victimized by society. And we know that when people feel powerless, they may tend to lash out. Our teenage boys are not immune to this tendency.

Now, you may feel quite strongly that you have raised a good boy with solid values and an unwavering moral code. Of course, you feel that you have. But these Voices are impervious to your parenting. They are opportunists, working in ways designed specifically to radicalize your teenage boys and young men into cult-like thinking. They are convincing boys—rather readily—that everyone who is not us is part of a group of "others," and that the mission of those others is to marginalize us, weaken us, and take from us what is rightfully ours. I can imagine that this is difficult to read, and that it's even more difficult to believe that your guy could play any part in it. But I've worked with boys who are sweet, thoughtful, and kind who stun me with the hateful, misogynistic, or racist comments that come out of them. Think of the Voices as being like your parents watching a fear-based twenty-four-hour news channel. You hear enough about fear, and you become fearful. The same principle applies to our boys. They hear enough about hate and scarcity, and they become hateful, radicalized, and even brainwashed to an extent.

The good news is that I find that a bit of discussion and debate can open a young man's mind quite readily. I've engaged in these discussions in my therapy office, and I've witnessed parents doing the same with their teenage sons. I'll caution you that bringing this up can be a touchy thing. You need to ensure that you are not shaming him when you present other points of view, and you need to fully hear him out and let him know that you understand his thoughts and feelings, even if you don't share them.

Expert Tip: Hear for Yourself

Sit down with your son and ask him about some of the Voices. Listen to a podcast with him or watch some of his favorite YouTube videos. Check out his TikTok and his Snapchat. Take a few minutes in the car when you're together to listen to some of the music he likes. There are a number of benefits to your attention here. First, your guy will see that you are showing an interest in his interests, and that's a solid deposit in the emotional bank account you have with him.

But there are other benefits as well. You will have a better understanding of the Voices he's listening to, the Voices that shape his thinking about the world, himself, others, and even his future. I will warn you that you will learn that your son is likely listening to voices that will surprise you, and ones that you disagree with completely. But you need to know in order to weigh in. And that's the next benefit. You should ask your son what he thinks of what he hears and listen to his perspective carefully.

Is he open-minded and curious? Is he angry? Is there hate in his developing thought patterns? It may seem a strange set of questions, but trust me, they are relevant. And only when you understand can you offer him your perspective in a manner in which *your* voice will be truly heard and considered. Otherwise, you'll be readily dismissed as not understanding, or in some cases, it may seem to him as if you don't

even care enough to understand. You definitely want to avoid giving
him that impression, because he matters to you.

Your input here is crucial. It can influence your young man's thinking
enormously. But it's important to remember how intelligent and
discerning he is. You cannot simply tell him how to think. Instead,
have an honest conversation with him. Share your point of view.
Allow him some space to weigh that against the Voices, in order to
find his own.

Some context is important here so that you as parents understand
some of what your boys are experiencing. First, we need to recognize
that there is an awful lot of the internal lives of our boys and young
men we know very little or nothing about. Much of what they take
in is invisible to us. Their belief systems, thoughts, and ideas take
shape and are supported behind a closed door, or right next to us
through earbuds.

So, I've asked our guys about their influences, and they have cited
certain men over and over and over again. These men are: Joe Rogan,
Jordan Peterson, Russell Brand, Andrew Tate, Dave Portnoy, and of
course, Donald Trump.

There are others, to be sure. And I am not going to spend a lot of
time judging these men. I'm not sure they're out to recruit your
boys into an army that's anti-female, anti-government, or against
LGBTQIA+ people.

Any such hateful messaging can be dangerous. But these men carry
loud, persistent megaphones that infiltrate the thinking of *so* many of
our boys. Rogan can run a podcast for four hours. Our boys will listen.
It's fun; it's compelling and interesting; it's entertaining. The vast
majority of those four hours are benign, even enriching. But you need

to know that this is one of a number of voices shaping the thinking of our boys and young men. And there are others.

Jordan Peterson is smart and sharp and well-spoken. He has the respect of a lot of boys. How can this educated and experienced professor—of psychology of all things—be mistaken?

And Dave Portnoy heads Barstool, the largest sports franchise outside ESPN. This guy's fun. He's a sports guy. We agree with him about the Eagles defense, so why wouldn't we agree that our voices are being silenced if he's telling us that as well?

The misogyny, hate, and bitterness that are permeating our culture can be drawn from these voices, even if these men do not all intend for that to happen. I know this is true. Boys and young men share these thoughts with me week after week and have done so for years. Again, these voices can be in the heads of our boys and young men for several hours every single day. There is no lack of content for them to consume, and sometimes, they tell me, the content finds them—in a notification, in the middle of watching a TV show, in a pop-up ad on YouTube, or even in the middle of a video game.

The rabbit hole is not just deep. It's never-ending.

Case study: Kyle

Kyle is a very cool, unique kid. He started coming to me at age sixteen, complaining of symptoms of depression and anxiety. Kyle is kind, engaging and funny. He's a smart kid who knows a lot about a lot, from music to sports to politics and philosophy.

In a moment of exceptionally keen self-awareness, Kyle overtly recognized that he himself is a work in progress. He knows he has strong feelings regarding philosophy, politics, gender, faith, and masculinity. He gets that his frontal lobe at this age is not fully developed, and that much of what he *thinks* he believes may represent a combination of other factors as well, including raging hormones and a not-yet-fully-developed brain. Think about the insight it must take to realize that about yourself. I know I didn't possess this awareness at Kyle's age.

Also, consider for a moment the flexibility in thinking required to recognize that although you may believe in something strongly now, it is fully possible that when presented with a different set of data or a more relevant point of view, your mind may change. All of this is to point out with clarity the good news hidden underneath the alarm bells: Like Kyle, many of our boys and young men are actually quite open-minded, perhaps even more so than many of us. So, when they sense dissonance, even within some of what they feel to be their core beliefs, many of them carry enough ego strength to admit they're wrong and to make corrections in their points of view.

However, I find that when these young men feel pressed into positions of becoming ideologues in order to have a voice, that flexibility is quickly eradicated. The fix, Kyle would tell us, is open-minded discussion. His parents are good listeners and tend to validate his point of view as legitimate. On occasion, however, they'll challenge him. Kyle tells me he loves these types of dialogues with his parents. He feels respected and open to learning because the conversation is not a one-sided lecture.

And this is precisely what our boys need to counterbalance the dark voices that are vying for their attention and perhaps their very identities. In order to be heard in the minds of our boys, we need to listen as well.

Case Study: The LGBTQ Community

It's critical, and often even a matter of life and death, that we encourage our boys to be supportive of their LGBTQ peers. Many of the Voices that populate the media our boys consume are critical of LGBTQ people; some are dismissive of this community, and some want to ignore its presence altogether.

There's this interesting dichotomy among young people. I find that when I ask their opinions in an environment free of the Voices, almost all of them have wide-open minds. I've worked with many boys who have said that it's important, regardless of gender identity or sexual preference, that they are supportive of their peers.

But some of the Voices that I have discussed here provide very different and sometimes dangerous messages. The most harrowing and awful messages, both boys and girls tell me, involve the trans community. Some of the pervasive ideas articulated by the Voices include the reactionary allegations that transgender people are grooming young people or merely posing as transgender in order to get into the bathrooms of the opposite gender.

I suspect I don't have to tell you that both the larger LGBTQ community and the transgender community in particular are highly susceptible to severe emotional difficulties. A shocking percentage of transgender people attempt suicide and complete it. If you have a child who is transgender, you may have tried to talk him out of it for this very reason because you are afraid for them.

I've worked with kids who are gay, lesbian, bisexual, transgender, and queer. Like all the kids I work with, they are to a person amazing individuals. They have big spirits and important voices of their own that we need to create space for. In this text, we are talking primarily about boys. But if your son or your daughter comes to you questioning their gender identity or sexual preference, it is absolutely critical that you listen to them and believe them. I assure you they are not bringing this up to test your acumen as a parent. They are not bringing it up because it was suggested to them on Snapchat or is a trend. Most of the LGBTQ kids I work with say that their path in life is more difficult because they are gay, transgender, or queer.

And it's important to note that I work with far, far too many kids who are terrified about how their parents are going to feel about the reality of their identity. Many feel hopeless and as if they have nowhere to turn. They tend to confide in the their receptive friends who have not been indoctrinated by biased Voices.

As parents, our job here is clear. Be fully supportive of your child. Remember that your child isn't a different person because they recognize they are gay, queer, or transgender. That is still your child, your brilliant child, recognizing with more clarity who he, she, or they are. Your support here is crucial. It can be lifesaving.

Now, as a final note, I should say that on occasion, I do work with some kids who are confused about either their sexual identity or who they are drawn to in a romantic way. This is a particular parenting challenge, as the straight road tends to be the easiest. But that child needs to know you're supportive of whoever they are as well as the process of determining who they are. The anguish some of these kids suffer for fear of what their parents will feel about them is well beyond anything any of you would want your kid to go through. So, I urge you with every breath I've got to partner and collaborate with them on this journey. In doing so, you can help make a difficult thing far, far easier. And sometimes, you can experience enormous joy together through this process.

Masculinity Confusion

"Girls go for a-holes. People are drawn to pervy, douchebag dudes. There's literally no incentive to be a nice guy, or even a decent person."

—David, seventeen

When I started in this profession twenty-five years ago, the distinction between masculine and feminine felt abundantly clear, as clearly distinct as blue and pink, for better or worse. In the past several years, it seems to me that femininity and feminism have come into sharper focus with increased attention on the rights and freedoms of girls and women. I've asked a number of young people what the word feminine means to them, and their responses were clear. Femininity is comprised of a number of qualities, including emotional intelligence, empathy, compassion, communication, and sensitivity.

The same makeshift survey showed on the other hand that we are running into competing and conflicting notions of masculinity. Is masculinity a show of physical strength and sexual prowess, as it has been defined in previous eras? Or is it possible that masculinity can now inhabit more dimensions? Can the rough-and-tumble we see in boys coexist with emotional language and expressiveness? Can boys and young men be both strong and vulnerable? Is there room for gentleness in the lives of our boys?

Many of my confused young male clients ask me what it means to be *masculine*.

In recent years, our boys have been taught that the very nature of masculinity is *toxic*. The term toxic masculinity is common in our culture, and our boys come across the term virtually everywhere they look: in their Twitter feeds, in memes and GIFs shared on TikTok, or in conversation with friends or family. I urge you to stop and consider this for a moment. Boys come into my office for initial sessions, and the idea that they were born toxic is already deeply embedded in many of their minds. They have carried this idea in one way or another for years at that point.

Boys exhibit so much confusion about masculinity. They see something in their fathers, in the way they dress and smell and work, that reads as masculine to them. Dads have been described to me as strong, tough, temperamental, removed, and stoic. In the same breath, many, many young men have shared with me that they do not wish to be like their fathers, at least not in every way. They typically describe their dads as their childhood heroes. But as they get to know them as men, they realize there is something missing in the lives of their fathers that they are in no hurry to replicate, but that they fear is hard-wired into their DNA.

They see that, far too often, their fathers are disconnected and lonely. They have few close, personal relationships. They have few hobbies or interests they pursue, so too often, from a boy's point of view, his father's life seems far too devoid of passion. Fathers too often do work that is uninteresting, draining, and uninspired, and most do not hide this—they are vocal about their career disappointments. Their sons have taken notice and are confused about the nature of men's work. Is it supposed to be grueling? Are they supposed to enjoy it, or simply endure it? Should they find meaning in it? Or is it just drudgery?

Questions like this settle in the minds of young men, and eventually, many of them lose direction. They are not sure where to place their energies, and this is the point at which much of the opting out of their lives takes root. Why go to class if it leads to unhappiness? Why try if I'm not making a difference? And even if I'm successful, whatever that means, do I want the life my father has? Far too often, the boys I work with say no.

And I'll remind you that fathers remain the primary role models for boys and young men. So, in the light of these observations, hopelessness and despair about the nature of masculinity and about their own futures often settle in far too early in life for our boys.

We all remember the ill-fated day of January 6, 2021, when the US Capitol building was under siege, along with the lawmakers inside. A large and unwieldy group, mostly made up of men, overpowered the small police force on the premises and breached the building and eventually the chambers of the House as well. We are all aware of the violence that ensued and the threats that were made, but one moment in particular made a powerful impression on me, so much so that I watched it over and over again.

One man, the self-proclaimed "QAnon Shaman," stood in the back of the House chamber and howled loudly and assertively, an act that to me smacked of an almost primal masculine message: We are winning. We are conquering. We need to finish the job. He seemed to be declaring victory over something with the howl, and I found myself eagerly curious to see what happened next.

Well, he marched around the large chamber for a couple of minutes with authority, riffling through papers and flipping over a couple of chairs. Slowly, the rest of the group seemed to lose interest in any authority he may have had and went about their own looting and threatening without him. Within five minutes of the howl, this man was in the Speaker's seat, asking another man to take a pic of him there with his phone and send it to him.

Of course, all of those people who threatened our democracy that day deserve to be prosecuted to the fullest extent of the law. But this moment struck me as uniquely pathetic, a man realizing in real time the degree to which he had misconstrued and bastardized masculinity. He felt what he had been taught was the epitome of masculine power, yet within minutes, he recognized the degree to which he was entirely powerless. The concept of masculinity he had been taught was toxic, to be sure, and left him with absolutely nothing to show for it, save for maybe a jail stint and a Wikipedia footnote as a national joke. Toxic masculinity is just a pathetic, empty, cartoon cutout of who a man is "supposed" to be. But it has nothing at all to do with what masculinity truly is. The distinction is an important one.

I think we have a unique opportunity for our boys and young men at this moment in history. We have the chance to help redefine the nature of masculinity. I would propose that we add to it. A man can be strong, but let's clarify what we mean by that word. Let's consider whether some of the traditionally feminine qualities can also be encompassed in our definition of masculinity. Can vulnerability be a sign of strength? How about sensitivity and empathy? Kindness? Social connection skills? How about emotional expression?

Consider a man you admire and think of moments with him that most drew your admiration. Was he distant and stoic in those moments? Or was he showing you some true self, a kind, thoughtful, gentle, and compassionate man? Most of us would say that's precisely the kind of man we want to raise. But to do so, we have to be intentional in our parenting. We have to provide our sons with some blueprint for this type of life.

Expert Tip: Addressing Toxic Masculinity

Through my work with young people, I've been finding that, more and more, the concepts of masculinity and femininity are not blurred so much as combined. Young people seem to be organically drawing from the best of the traditionally feminine traits and integrating them with masculine traits in order to truly discover the full extent of their character and personalities. I need to note that they do so with no small degree of blowback from older generations.

I work with a seventeen-year-old boy I'll call Tyler, an exceptionally cool and insightful kid who abhors black-and-white thinking but thoroughly enjoys integrating ideas, sometimes including ideas that seem initially to clash with one another. He feels there are important distinctions between men and women, but that we are at our best when we are both strong and soft, tough yet kind, book smart, street smart, and emotionally smart. Tyler recognizes that, at seventeen, he can only know so much for sure. So, he reads a lot. He listens to a lot of podcasts. And through all of what he takes in, he tries to discern his truth.

Tyler stumbled upon a podcast about the divine feminine and told me he listened to it a couple of times, rapt. Feeling that nobody needs to corner the market on divinity, he proposed that we create a form of the divine masculine that covers guys like him, sensitive and athletic, empathic and curious. In this session in my office, he realized that with every adjective he was using to define himself, he was also describing his sister, his girlfriend, and his mom. Maybe, he suggested, the best of what is masculine and feminine is the best of all of us.

I believe he's right. Further, I think if we shed those parts of us that are deemed toxic, we will realize those are really just our emotional pain in disguise.

That's masculine. That's feminine. That's strength and love. Man, that's everything.

Toxic Masculinity

I recently read a *New York Times* piece about the trope of the TV dad. It has been argued that in both sitcoms and dramas of the past, "Dad" was portrayed as a caricature, a buffoon lacking in work ethic, parenting skill, common sense, and perhaps most subtly yet pointedly at the same time, emotional intelligence. From Homer Simpson to Archie Bunker to Peter Boyle to Ray Barone, the sitcom dad has historically been a joke, and sometimes the sole plotline, episode by episode, was Dad trying to avoid getting in trouble with Mom, typically ending up foiled in the end.

The depiction of men in dramas tends to be more understated. Dad has more dimension, and his crankiness is explained either overtly or in flashback. Still, he typically just doesn't get it, or requires extensive coaching to foster a meaningful, supportive moment. Even today, in many of the dramas in the age of Netflix, women are the arbiters of judgment, virtue, and kindness. Mom may nod approvingly as she benevolently eavesdrops on Dad's rare connecting moment from another room.

It is noteworthy that men and boys tend to be portrayed as idiots in the very material boys and young men consume. They are watching *Family Guy* and *It's Always Sunny in Philadelphia* on loop, unwittingly supporting the narrative of the hapless, emotionally dopey male.

One might argue that this portrayal is relatively innocuous and has perhaps even been an effort to even out the playing field a bit, given that men hold so much power in our society. In most of these programs, in fact, one can reasonably guess that men served as writers, producers, and directors as well as leading actors. Maybe it's only fair they play the fools.

But the language we use around men and boys has shifted quite a bit in recent years, and it's become far less funny and far more serious. In the wake of the #MeToo movement, the term toxic masculinity has become omnipresent in nearly every cultural conversation, including, I'm told, every high school and college class that touches on gender— and even many of those that do not.

This term is toxic unto itself for a number of reasons. First, I have found that many, many boys and young men come into my office for initial sessions feeling as if toxicity is a fundamental component of who they are. Some of these boys are just entering puberty, and that drain on their sense of self-worth is potent. They feel badly about themselves and question their own motives to the point where many of them feel they cannot trust their own thoughts and sensibilities. What's worse, they often come into these formative years resenting girls and women for seeing them through this lens, perpetuating a negative narrative that may not apply to all boys and men.

This is precisely where we really need to be surgically accurate with the language we use. No boy is born toxic. This is a crucial idea that all of us need to internalize. Their behavior may prove to be toxic at times, and that needs to be addressed without question. Too many girls, women, boys and men, and others have fallen victim to that toxic and even violent and threatening behavior. It is unacceptable, every time, regardless of circumstances—period.

But boys cannot successfully begin their adult lives with the belief that they are inherently toxic. As a clinician, I can tell you that this belief diminishes the self-worth of boys.

The distinction is critical, as is the resulting behavioral fallout. If a boy believes he is toxic to women and to society, a number of things can happen. He may be prone to inaction for fear of hurting others. He may isolate for the same reason. Or, on the other hand, he may lash out in anger at this label, whether the labeling is implied or overt. He may in fact hurt someone.

He may be the boy who pushes a girl beyond her comfort level sexually. He may be the boy who brings a loaded gun to school to prove his detractors right. He may become the modern-day cult leader, spreading hate speech like a virus on a podcast directed at other boys and young men. It doesn't take a lot of foresight to recognize that a belief that one is inherently toxic may become the ultimate self-fulfilling prophecy.

Our language matters.

Expert Tip: Shift the Language

If you are a parent or other influential adult in the life of a boy or young man, sit down and talk with them about this language. You don't need to be overly cautious or concern yourself with the idea that you're introducing this language to your guy for the first time. I've worked with enough young people to assure you that this seed has already been planted in their young brains many times over. Talking about it openly will help in and of itself.

So, to get him to think differently about himself, offer him your impressions of him. Provide him with some of the positive adjectives and roles you see him playing. In every initial session with a young person and their parents, I ask Mom and Dad to briefly describe the difficulties and issues that bring them to therapy. But then I immediately ask them what they love about their son, what's special and unique and amazing about him.

These tend to be among the most beautiful, sacred, seminal moments I'm lucky enough to witness in a therapeutic setting. In most of these sessions, it quickly becomes apparent that these are not conversations my families share either openly or frequently, if ever at all. To watch buried emotions swell in all parties is a privilege, as well as a game changer for the family.

I've noticed that, in some of these sessions, parents feel some degree of discomfort, not because they don't feel fondness and admiration for their child, but because they are not accustomed to expressing it, especially not with an audience present. As you might guess, fathers are far more reluctant than mothers in this regard. After all, this doesn't fit under the umbrella we tend to label as masculine. We'll talk more about the language around masculinity in a moment.

In the meantime, I strongly urge you to press beyond that discomfort, even outside the structure of therapy, and tell your boy or young man how you feel about him. Let him know explicitly how much you love him, and take the time to delineate the reasons why. He may start with an eye roll, but eventually, you will get to him. He will hear you. And he will carry your words with him. I can assure you that you are in a unique position to provide him with another lens through which to view himself, one that is decidedly less noxious and more positive and progressive.

Your own language is super powerful here, more so than you might ever imagine. Your boy will not only listen to you but will integrate your reflections of him into his sense of self-worth. They need your words to counterbalance the negative language about boys they're assimilating from the greater culture, on playgrounds, in basements, or online.

Two final observations here. I find these discussions precious in part because I am fully aware, often in real time, that many families never, ever engage in this kind of emotional talk with one another. We are stingy with our praise, fondness, and admiration. This may be an artifact of a more stoic time during which many of us grew up. It may reflect a discomfort with intimate subject matter. Or it might represent a belief that by giving too much positive feedback, we are fueling a generation of self-absorbed, entitled brats and making them feel better about themselves without any distinct action on their part to earn it.

None of this is necessary, and most of it is based on dangerous fallacy. The passive, removed, unemotional style of parenting many of us grew up with may have worked to an extent at the time. But with the stressors our kids face now, there is absolutely no need to add to their burden. Just making it through these highly stressful times provides all the resilience your boys—and girls—will need to lean on for a lifetime. Adding to this is wholly unnecessary. I would far prefer you to focus on your connection with your child and on fostering a role as their ally, guide, and consultant through the troubled waters of adolescence and young adulthood.

As far as discussing intimate topics with your kids, you have simply got to get over it. In any given day online, your kids are exposed to intimate language. Via texting and on Snapchat, Instagram, and TikTok, kids trade in intimate language with one another. They frequently tell each other how much they love and value each other. This is often easy and joyful for them—second nature. If you're *not* engaging in these types of discussions with your kids, you're missing out on some beautiful conversations with them that can have results which are far from frivolous. So yes, get over it. If doing so changes the culture of your family, it will be for the better, believe me. This may prove awkward at first, but stick with it. Over time, these talks will feel increasingly natural.

Let's touch on the fallacy of this "entitled, self-centered generation" for just a moment. I can certainly see where some of us acquire that notion. Our kids take selfies. They are glued to their phones or some other screen far too often. They often disappear into their bedrooms, only entering common areas for food or to watch the big screen. I understand how it looks.

But I urge you to put yourself into the mind of your child, male, female, or otherwise, for just a moment. They have by far more academic and social pressure than we ever had to manage. They also need to maintain multiple personas, managing online identity traffic in order to sustain or gain social traction or just remain in the game socially. They also carry all of the information—literally all of it, good, bad, gory, and even pornographic—on the screens they hold in the palm of their hand. So, in the years when their attention should be focused on personal developmental milestones such as establishing a unique sense of self, unlike in previous generations, many kids are concerned instead with climate change, war refugees, clean water, or hunger, global issues that consume their minds while they're trying to accomplish all the usual tasks of adolescence and young adulthood. All of this is to say, it's different now. We cannot treat it as if it's the same as it's always been.

Secondly, this is not an intervention we need to reserve just for our boys. In different ways, all of our kids, including our girls, carry some negative feelings about themselves that permeate their sense of self-identity. Your honest reflections of their positive characteristics can serve as an antidote to the lion's share of this negative language. Do not do this sparingly, but speak positively to your child about how you feel about them until you feel as if you're fully heard, understood, and believed.

It's a big deal. If you follow no other recommendations offered here, follow this one. You will likely change the trajectory of your child's life, no small thing unto itself. But you will also be contributing to a positive shift in the cultural narrative around boys and men, a shift that will allow them to feel entitled to a seat at the table, and one that may create a societal win-win for all of us.

Just get started with more openly expressive emotional language, even if it makes you feel uncomfortable.

Sidebar: The Boss—The Strength of an Open Heart

If you have followed my work for any period of time, you know that I am a fan of availability in parenting, a style free of our own fear, judgment, and ego. You know that I believe our kids are being raised with a set of stressors most of us could never have imagined during our own adolescence. And you are very likely aware that I'm an unabashed Bruce Springsteen fan.

Since I was sixteen years old and stood for four hours on a Tuesday night with the shocking force and power and beauty and joy of rock and roll coursing through my very soul, I've been a Springsteen fan. He has always seemed the quintessential "alpha" to me: loud, muscular, strong, powerful, and brazenly unforgiving. I felt alive that night in a way I never have before, and in the decades since, I've taken in Bruce and the band live at every opportunity I've had to recapture that raw, masculine energy.

Seeing Bruce solo, on the other hand, has always been a particular
dream of mine. Then a few years ago, to my shock, Bruce decided to
put a one-man show up on Broadway. A sort of performance piece
based on the arc of his life, spanning from growing up the child of a
deeply troubled and depressed father to becoming a massive rock star
with a profound loneliness issue and starting a family of his own, it was
a beautiful piece interwoven with precious acoustic performances of
his most intimate music.

And this very personal Bruce, the one getting choked up talking about
his dad, the Bruce who speaks through the more emotional parts of
"My Hometown," "Independence Day," and even "Born to Run," who
reveals himself as a deeply flawed man, this Bruce is the one who really
moved me. Experiencing the wall of sound of an inspired rock band
along with fifty thousand like minds is a thrill, without a doubt. But
my respect for the man there alone on the stage, baring his soul to us
seemingly one by one, *this* guy I feel I know and respect.

And curiously, there is a strength in the sweetness, in the silence, and
in the honesty and vulnerability. Brené Brown has made a career of
pointing out, correctly I believe, that our vulnerability is our greatest
strength. In those moments on that stage, often clearly near tears,
Bruce could not have seemed *stronger*.

But this is not what we teach our boys about strength. And by the
time they become teenagers and young men, this current generation
of boys is wondering what strength really is and what elements of
their character comprise masculinity. If it's not the removed stoicism
presented by their fathers, who are they supposed to be as men? It's no
wonder they're confused.

And that's why we need to redefine masculinity for our boys. We need
to offer them permission to open up and be the people they *already*

are! I know that if we do so, we will see a precipitous drop in anxiety, depression, attention issues, suicidal thinking, and hopelessness in our boys and young men.

Who's Allowed at the Table?

The voice can take an unpredictable form. I was talking with a friend recently who overheard the following from moms of teenage sons in a locker room:

> "I told Bobby that this is not your time. This is my time. This is your sister's time. This is a time for you to step back and allow space for girls and women to step up. This. Is not. Your time."

Now, these are the words of a highly educated, deeply loving mother to her teenage son. If we take a moment to consider it, it's not too difficult to understand what she means. Girls and women have waited a long, long time for this moment.

But here's the thing we all need to recognize about the Voices. The Voices have a point, and they know it and exploit it regularly. They recognize that our boys, too, have in a way been silenced. They have been shamed. Culturally, for the past several years of their lives, as the #MeToo movement and the cancel culture and women's marches and female empowerment have taken center stage in our headlines, many of them feel shame solely because of their gender.

Now, it's often said that it's a man's world. After all, men continue to lead the vast majority of corporate America. Men control Wall Street and its self-aggrandizing, "too big to fail" corruption. A man has ended up sitting in the White House after every single election.

No doubt, it's a man's world.

But is it really?

The girls and women I see in my practice are powerful, strong, and hopeful. They see the glass ceiling breaking, and they can envision the opportunities opening up for them in a very bright future. Many of them have told me so: Even in their darkest moments, they see slivers of light that can empower them and light their way.

And women are supporting other women like never before.

There are also elements of our culture, once dominated almost solely by men, which are now the bastion of women: smart women; powerful women; role models proclaiming they will no longer be silenced, that they have something to say.

There are few places I love more than an airport bookstore. I love to grab a new story and take it with me, adding to my real-world adventure. I love to scan the titles and book jackets, excitedly seeking out the possibilities of story and character and failure and redemption and mystery just waiting to be revealed.

Before one recent trip, as I scanned author names on a bookstore shelf, I came upon another revelation. More and more, bestselling books, both fiction and nonfiction, are written by women. I read women writers almost exclusively. Oprah, Reese Witherspoon, and Jenna Bush select excellent titles for their book clubs, titles written primarily by women.

In sports, athletes like Simone Biles and Naomi Osaka can increasingly make headlines right alongside LeBron James and Roger Federer.

I began to think about the music and podcasts I listen to—mostly women. Who do I trust as journalists and reporters? Who do I find funny, honest, authentic, and intelligent?

Mostly women.

I believe the most powerful influences shaping our culture right now are women, hands down.

It's a far more Glennon Doyle and Brené Brown world than an outdated Tony Robbins world. It's been happening right under our noses in a truly beautiful and elegant way for years.

And for the record, I am 100 percent behind this movement. I hope it never ends. I love to see the light of hope in the eyes of the girls I work with, the promise of a far better and more inclusive world, one in which their talents are deeply and honestly valued, not in a "let's even the score" way, but more in a "we *need* these voices and this energy in the world" way, strong yet peaceful, mighty and empathic, talented and emotionally honest and vulnerably powerful.

But the problem is, our boys and young men do not feel they have a seat at the table. On the contrary, they don't feel as if they've earned it nor that they deserve it. As in the quote above, they are hearing it is not their time. They are part of the gender that has created all of the problems and cultural difficulties we deal with. It's time for them to sit down, get away from the table, and shut up.

And they have been taught that they lack all of these stereotypically "feminine" qualities outlined above.

But these qualities are not absent in them. The best of our boys and young men shows up in them when they are at their most open and vulnerable and emotionally intelligent and present. In the same breath, however, we have taught them that these are not the hallmarks of masculinity. Those are stoicism, solitary self-reliance, and exerting power *over*, not *with*, others.

Just imagine the confusion of these boys. They feel like they need to shapeshift based on their audience, and therefore they may never listen to that inner voice that tells them who they are. Believe me, as a clinician working with boys and young men for a generation, this inner conflict is a real one. It drives a lot of the anxiety, depression, and opting out our boys exhibit on a more and more regular basis every day.

In fact, I feel a bit of imposter syndrome as I write these words now. I am a therapist, writer, and speaker. I am a privileged white male writing on an international flight to a dream vacation. I am anxious that the woman sitting next to me might be side-eying my screen, taking in these words, and judging me as another mansplainer assuming he has something important to say. Maybe my time has come and passed. Maybe the likes of me have driven the problems I'm looking to help solve here in the first place. Perhaps I don't deserve a seat at the table.

I am also a man in a slice of the world dominated by women. Far more women than men are therapists. And among that group, the little subset that focuses on parenting is nearly all women. Perhaps it would be better for me to keep my white, middle-aged, toxic, privileged ideas to myself. Maybe one of my female colleagues is better equipped to be heard on this topic. And if I err here in any discernible way, maybe if I bow out and toss this manuscript, I can avoid getting humiliated and canceled for not being careful enough with my language. As I write, I am asking myself: Is this my message? Is it my book to write? To promote on a tour? To profit from?

Or should I slide my chair back from the table, shut up, and recognize it is not my time?

Remember, I'm a grown man with a long life behind me gaining experience, wisdom, and hopefully some insight, and I'm experiencing these thoughts and fears. With that in mind, just imagine how confusing these times must be for our boys.

Why Boys Need Seats at the Table

My hope is that this is a good time to be a girl and a woman in our culture, that the trend continues and the glass ceilings break ever more readily with each passing year.

But we have to be very aware of declaring winners and losers. To my thinking, if women win and are successful, and all of their strength and brilliance is absorbed by our society and utilized for the good that it brings, not only are women winning, but we are all winning. The world is a better place. Enormous problems that may seem to lack solutions, including the climate crisis, the lack of diplomacy between nations, and all those vast issues that make us humans a threat to ourselves can then better be solved.

But from the chair in my office, I can see that if this is a one-way street and we declare winners *and losers*, then we will usher in whole set of new problems, even if some of the old problems are resolved. Women *and* men, girls *and* boys, all need a seat at the table in order for our society to work the way it needs to. This is a micro problem to be sure, one that must be approached boy by boy and man by man. But this is a macro issue as well. Our entire society is at stake, and I think that given a moment's pause, we all know that to be true.

Remember that our boys have a great deal to offer as well, and the gifts, values, and abilities they carry may surprise you. It is not that we have to channel their aggressive tendencies to show our collective strength. That's not where their strength lies. Like girls, our boys are also deeply emotional and empathic. With each passing year, I'm finding the boys I work with to be ever kinder, more thoughtful, less tolerant of cruelty and bullying, and more tolerant of individual differences. There's a lot of power in these attributes.

We don't have to dim one light to brighten another. They can all shine bright.

Expert Tip: Room for Everyone

I had a conversation with my family recently about scarcity and abundance. The scarcity thinkers out there may be thinking that life is a zero-sum game, that there is only so much of the good stuff to go around: money, power, influence, comfort. Scarcity thinking drives the "us vs. them" thinking that has dominated the US political system in the past several years and deepened divisions between parties, races, genders, and generations.

I don't always practice the idea that the good things in life are abundant, but in this situation, I know it's a reality. There is a synergy when the best in all of us is allowed a seat at the table. When we are all allowed to express ourselves, regardless of who we are or how we present, only good can result from that. And deep down, I think we would all agree that everyone—each and every person—is valuable. I believe it's with that thinking in mind that we can find space for women, men, girls, boys, and everyone else at the table.

A Call to Action

I've been speaking to some men in my generation lately, asking them what the messaging was for us when we grew up. Their answers didn't surprise me and mirrored my experience growing up. Most guys said they were encouraged to be strong and studious and responsible. They were urged to "man up" and keep a stiff upper lip. Oh, and avoid crying, especially in public, because that's a big old sign of weakness.

Back then, we were also encouraged to run, and play, and work. We were pressed to participate in sports as fierce competitors.

Boys now receive similar messaging within the home. But it is complicated by the messages they receive outside the home, as well as on the phone screens, podcasts, and social media they constantly consume. Out there, they are told that they are the sexual assaulters and harassers. They are told males have no understanding of the resulting trauma because they lack the capacity for deep empathy. Boys are the school shooters, the angry and violent losers infected with hate. Men are the crooked politicians and soulless Wall Street businessmen. They have been the problem for too long. It is no longer their time. Now, their job is to sit quietly and support the girls in their lives, who have been paid too little attention and have been marginalized for decades, for centuries. Girls, boys are told, innately possess superior skills to manage themselves in a classroom. They don't misbehave. They care about other people. They're studious and disciplined. Boys, on the other hand, are messy and inattentive. They're problematic. They may need extra teacher attention or prescribed medication to make it through the school day.

This clash of messaging leaves boys feeling immobilized. They far too often feel powerless and hopeless.

And they come by these feelings honestly. I recently worked with a
brilliant young man, nineteen-year-old Ryan. Having worked very
hard in high school, Ryan gained admission to a highly prestigious
university. Once on campus, he decided he wanted to spend some
of his time understanding the difficulties for both kids and adults
of all genders in modern society. Given all the sweeping cultural
change around gender, he took a gender studies course just to better
understand the issues. The first few weeks, he learned a lot. He noted
that the vast majority of students in the class were female, and he
thought that should be rectified. He thought more guys his age should
be interested in what's going on in gender today.

But he also told me that in real time he sensed an undercurrent of
sentiment against men in this class. The girls and women in the class
were called on most frequently for discussion and questions. He noted
a lot of talk about toxic masculinity, and the societal problems caused
by men seeking to gain power, money, sex, or fame.

Ryan actually had some points he wished to make and some questions
to ask. He wanted to speak up frequently during each class. But every
time he thought about raising his hand, he stopped himself. The
risks of being called out, of being accused of not getting it, or of being
canceled in real time felt too great for him. Eventually, Ryan, who
again had chosen to take this course in order to better understand,
dropped the class altogether. To him, the risks outweighed any
potential rewards. And he was just too anxious in there to continue.

I want us to stop and consider Ryan's plight for just a moment. Here's
a young man intent on being part of the solution. He senses enough ill
will toward him for his very maleness and his perceived privilege that
he feels silenced as a result. Whatever brilliance he could have had to
offer in a gender studies class that may have had ripple effects in the
culture at large was stifled. He remains discouraged and disheartened

and fears he will always have to be cautious about what he says and does. For the rest of his life, he fears he will have to tread lightly around girls and women.

He is reluctant to date for fear of being called out for inappropriate behavior. He is even hesitant to work with women for fear of being misunderstood or saying the wrong thing and getting canceled in some way or another.

So, a young man who wants to help and learn steps back in line, silent and afraid.

This doesn't feel right, does it?

Recently, I was listening to Jon Stewart, whom I highly respect and admire not only as a man but as a *comedian*, on a podcast talking about what he termed the "cancer of cancel culture." In that moment, he was specifically speaking about himself and his peers—comedians—a group he deemed to be the last existing bastion of public truth. Specifically, he was talking about some of the bits that he and some other male counterparts in comedy no longer felt comfortable delivering to an audience. He pointed out, accurately I think, that if comedians feel silenced, our culture is in trouble. If we are not allowed to question authority, norms, and trends, we are in a dangerous position indeed.

Stewart correctly points out a need for a course correction here with a high degree of urgency. We all know that we are in turbulent times, politically, socially, economically, and otherwise. And if we cannot look at ideas from different points of view, and even from a comedic perspective, we are in trouble. We are forced into a kind of dangerous tunnel vision that eliminates a lot of important possibilities from our futures.

The only answer, Stewart claimed in the podcast, was a sea change in terms of open-mindedness and listening to all voices, even and perhaps especially those that we disagree with the most. We need to be willing to challenge our own thinking on convention and authority and gender and race and opportunity. If we're not willing to do that, we're going to miss the opportunity to collaboratively devise the solutions, and we simply cannot let that happen.

Like Ryan, like Stewart's comedians, our boys are being silenced, and that's not good for them. Along with feeling powerless and hopeless, many of the boys I have known and worked with are now feeling worse. Symptoms set in, symptoms like anxiety, depression, and suicidal thinking. This is far more common than most people know. As a clinician, I feel a distinct duty to report what I've been seeing in the therapy room that can inform our approach to boys and young men moving forward.

Because silencing is no good for our boys. It drains the life from their eyes and the hope from their futures. It leaves them either pent up, angry, and frustrated, or just deeply sad. None of this motivates our boys to engage in the world, to overcome their anxieties, and to offer the gifts they carry to the world. Instead, they lead somewhat clandestine lives. They hole up in basements or bedrooms or dorm rooms, whiling away their time on activities that are in their lives just to pass time. Believe me, if they are smoking weed all day long, or gaming morning to night, or always scrolling through social media or placing bets, there is no joy there. There may be a passing dopamine rush or a momentary high, but joy? No, they're not feeling that. So no, choosing silence and stifling themselves is not good for our boys.

But it's also important to note that it's not good for any of us. These boys are brothers and sons, and they may grow up to be future partners to women, and possibly even fathers of girls. One doesn't have to think too hard to recognize that if anyone in our society is silenced, if any group is marginalized and told they don't matter and are not important, such disenfranchisement inevitably leads to problems: resentment, revolt, and even possibly violence, inward or outward.

For our boys and young men, the problems are somewhat obvious. They not only feel rejected by the culture these days, but they are not allowed to contribute any strengths, talents, or wonderful ideas that they have. They become sullen and listless. Over time, they often become symptomatic, possibly depressed, and anxious. For some of them, the hopelessness affiliated with marginalization can lead to depressive thinking or worse.

And this is the stuff the drives what we are calling toxic masculinity. Through podcasts, YouTube programs, and other highly accessible venues, our boys are internalizing messages suggesting that something is being taken away from them. Because they are not being heard, and because they are being blamed for the sins of men who came before them, they are dismissed. We will talk about the Voices that deliver these messages, but for now, just know that they are loud, powerful, and front and center in our boys' minds an awful lot of the time—far more than any of us might think.

So far, none of this has been solved, soothed, or repaired. It's festering in almost every boy's mind, on every high school and college campus. This messaging is now being handed down to a new generation of boys, but it is now far more heavily loaded than before.

We can't be lazy in how we think about this. We have to realize how important all the dynamics of interaction between the genders are. On a micro level, everyone needs to feel valued for their thoughts, their compassion, their ideas, and their values. On a macro level, this is the only way we thrive as a society and as a country. If we create gender wars and divisiveness, long-standing problems will result that will never be solved. We will never get to the point where we're addressing the needs of the underprivileged, raising our collective standing on the world stage, implementing a real and workable approach to healthcare, and creating a vibrant economy that's supportive of everyone. We need to be clear with boys that we need them—their voices, their strength, their sensitivity.

There's a common idiom about the economy that suggests a rising tide lifts all boats. I think that applies here as well. We all benefit from the rising tide of shared thoughts and open debate of ideas, discussions that include all of us.

All of that is to say, just as we need our girls and young women to know we value them in every way, we also need the same for our boys and young men.

One final note might be important here. I do not deny at all and I'm fully aware that many, many men have been very bad actors toward women and toward each other. I'm not here to defend any man who has sexually, physically, or emotionally abused or caused harm to a woman or to any other human being. I am not defending men who have placed their egos before the needs of others. I am not defending any man who has used his power or influence to victimize women or others. All of this is indefensible.

But we can't lay those sins at the feet of our boys today. If we do, I fear we will be perpetuating a cycle of abuse for another generation, a cycle that will only gain steam from generation to generation. We have an opportunity, right now, to make a sweeping change here. Our boys today are more self-aware, socially aware, empathic, and truly interested in being part of solutions. We need to take them up on that. But in order to do so, we first need to provide space for them to find their footing, socially, emotionally, academically, physically, spiritually, and otherwise.

We need sweeping change in the way we see and engage with our boys both generally and collectively. We need to create major affirmation in the lives of our boys. I get the impression from the boys I work with that they rarely feel celebrated for who they are. Given the loaded messaging they absorb about maleness in general, it's no surprise they feel that way. They need to know that we value and care for them. We need to rally for them, perhaps literally. Their lives are at stake, honestly.

I know that sounds perhaps grave and overly dramatic, but I promise you that for some of our boys, it's true. And the lives of some of the people around them are also at stake. Deep down, we all know this is true. And with this transformative wave of affirmation of our young men, I can envision a massive healing taking place in them. I can see them gaining self-esteem and self-worth. I can see light coming back into faces that have dimmed. I can see them reconnecting, hugging, smiling. My God, I so want that for them. I know you do as well. It doesn't have to be a pie-in-the-sky dream. This can be a reality.

There is a note of good news that I need to offer you here. On the whole, although there are dark voices encouraging them to do so, the vast majority of our young boys do not carry resentment or ill will toward girls and women. They actually have enormous respect and affection for them. In fact, many of the boys in my practice have expressed a desire to be as emotionally self-expressive and free as their female counterparts. They see the strength in that openness and vulnerability, and they want that for themselves. So, I don't want to leave you with the wrong idea here. We are not beyond the tipping point. Many boys fear connecting with girls, but they do continue to have a reverence for them. Many have told me that, given the courage and opportunity, they suspect they would connect far better with girls than guys. All is not yet lost. The opportunity for change remains.

Boy Behavior

We can look at recent cultural events that shape the feelings of lost young men, to be sure. As indicated earlier, the #MeToo movement certainly provided messaging that this is not the time for the young man or boy, especially the white young man or boy. But in order to truly understand the plight of our boys now, we have to go back in time and think back very far upstream.

Over the years, I've asked my young clients about their lives to date and when certain life events started to take place. The results were startling. Boys and girls recounted similar stories about their early years. Specifically, the fidgety, talkative, curious, mobile boys were labeled a problem once they were in a classroom with strict rules about behavior. Many were labeled behavior problems, and teachers have shared with me that they talk about which kids—in particular, which boys—are going to be a problem from grade to grade. Reputations can precede boys simply for being boys with each passing grade.

Then, almost as if by magic, an apparent solution for boy behavior presented itself, a solution which made boys fall in line and follow the guidelines rather more easily. This solution came in the guise of an established diagnosis in the *Diagnostic and Statistical Manual for Mental Disorders (DSM-5)*: Attention Deficit Hyperactivity Disorder, or what we all now refer to as ADD or ADHD.

Treatments that followed on this "breakthrough" diagnosis made an almost immediate impact on the behavior of children, boys especially, and allowed classrooms and other structured settings to function more smoothly, with fewer kids drawing attention away from the class, fewer calls from teachers or administrators to parents, and less strife at home. Also, the diagnostic bar for ADHD was strikingly low. If you have trouble attending to certain tasks to the degree to which it impacts your level of functioning, you have pretty well met the criteria. In actual practice, typical "boy behavior" was immediately pathologized and was often seen as requiring "treatment."

Special programming was developed in schools to accommodate for ADHD-diagnosed pupils, including longer times on tests and assignments and private spaces for test-taking if indicated. But these allowances required extensive meetings with all of a child's teachers, deans and other administrators, and outside therapists. They necessitated the availability of teachers and proctors to initiate and conduct these programs. In the end, they proved costly and unwieldy, especially for the overtaxed and underfunded public school systems across the country.

Years later, the pharmaceutical industry developed a wealth of stimulant medication to manage the symptoms of ADHD. You're likely familiar with several of these medications, from Adderall and Ritalin to Focalin and others. You very likely know several children taking them daily, most likely boys. You may have a child on one of these stimulants yourself.

And man, unlike most any other psychotropic medications, these meds fulfilled their promise. These were quickly regarded as miracle drugs that were stunning in their efficacy. Previously unfocused kids were in fact able to focus more efficiently for hours on end. And, if the effects wore off over the course of the day, and the daydreaming and fidgeting began to rear their heads again, low-dose boosters were available to bring your child back into focus. I was practicing when these medications became popular. Once medicated, I was struck by the degree to which "bad behavior" was managed in kids, usually boys in my experience, by a broad margin. And such a high percentage of my clients were quickly put on medication. It was a rapid, vast, and sweeping shift that continues to this day.

From my perspective, however, a couple of issues arise with this diagnosis and these medications. First, boys in particular are taught, unintentionally I believe, a couple of things when they are diagnosed. First, their organic behavior, the inclination to move, to talk, to joke, was *mis*-behavior, a problem to be solved. In essence, from a very young age, far too many boys have been taught to believe that they are bad and that the way they instinctively acted was unacceptable.

Second, as the frequency of diagnoses and prescriptions has risen, far too many boys have been left feeling not only as if they are behaving badly, but as if they lack the tools to correct or manage their behavior on their own. Quite the contrary, a prescription is necessary, suggesting they are "sick" or "afflicted." Many boys have told me they could never manage their bad behavior without their meds. Incidentally, many also said their medication made them feel weird or flat and unlike themselves. When you think about the symptoms these medications target, this makes quite a bit of sense, doesn't it?

This phenomenon is far more dangerous than it may at first appear to be. It establishes a mindset suggesting incompetence, and that can leave any child feeling he lacks the capability or grit to manage his behavior or any discomfort or stress without outside intervention. This has left a generation of boys feeling badly about themselves at just the developmental level where a sense of self is being established. Further, it leaves them unsure of their ability to handle those difficulties themselves and makes them question their own resilience.

I recently conducted a de facto poll of my young clients, asking them
what percentage of their male grammar school classmates they would
guess had been diagnosed with ADHD and prescribed a stimulant.
The estimates ranged from 50 to 80 percent, an alarming number even
to me. The ADHD craze has also vastly increased boys' identification
with psychiatric diagnoses as a core part of their sense of self:

- "I can't pay attention in class. I have ADHD."
- "I'll never feel better because I'm a depressive."
- "Some days, I'm just too anxious to go to school."

If all of this represents a significant part of a boy's belief system about
himself, one can imagine it impacts his self-image in a profoundly
negative way. I have learned this from far too many of my therapy
clients. In fact, many of them agree that the ADHD phenomenon
inevitably leads to the proliferation of excessive marijuana use by
teenage boys, much of it self-medication. They often smoke or vape
to manage their symptoms of anxiety, since many of them have been
trained to believe that any discomfort or diagnosis necessitates some
kind of medication. Too many have been conditioned to believe they
are neither capable nor resilient enough to manage or tolerate even
mild symptoms of attention difficulties, anxiety, or depression.

One interesting fact: The psychiatrist who first came up with the
ADHD diagnosis has since expressed regret for doing so, for many of
the reasons detailed here.

One final note is necessary here. I am not discounting the ADHD
diagnosis altogether. Quite the contrary: I've referred many young
clients struggling with true attention issues to psychiatrists, and
medication has improved the quality of their lives enormously.
Because the diagnostic bar is so low, however, the vast majority of
children prescribed these stimulant medications do not need them,

and many are worse off for taking them. And again, the vast majority of affected children are boys.

So, as you can see, we absolutely tend to pathologize typical boy behavior. And I can assure you that this follows some boys into young adulthood. Not long ago I worked with a college boy, Alan, who is struggling with the adjustment from high school to college. He was anxious, depressed, sad and lonely. He missed his friends from high school and the esteem he shared with his peers there. He realized he was self-medicating far too frequently with alcohol and marijuana.

His parents, however, found his behavior to be incredibly frustrating. They provided him with a fixed and fairly predictable set of options: Do better in school, get a part-time job, sign yourself into a psychiatric ward to fix your problems, or we kick you out of the house. In a session recently, Allen reported these stipulations, reflecting, "They don't care about me. They clearly want to get rid of me unless I'm perfect. Or if they do care, they certainly don't know how to show it."

Allen loves his parents, and he really needs their support in his life right now. But this impasse has severed the connection between them. He doesn't feel like they understand or listen. They just focus on his behavior, behaviors they don't support. He would also say they are behaviors they don't understand.

We talked about what Allen could do to improve this situation. He wasn't thrilled about it, but he agreed to go home and tell his parents how difficult of a time he has been having. He said this would be the first time that he was emotionally open with them, and he was really, really anxious about it. He thought they were going to kick him out on the spot.

Luckily, Allen's parents came through. They heard him out, and they came up with a couple of decisions together. Allen would withdraw from his classes for the semester. He would focus on his mental, emotional, and physical health. And his parents would be supportive.

I want you to keep in mind that not every young man is as self-aware and open as Allen. That is, when your guy is experiencing a challenging time, even if he is an adult, he may not come to you with his difficulties. He may feel they are a sign of weakness, or that you will see them as such. He may not have the emotional self-awareness to know what's going on with him or what's stopping him from performing better in school or at home. So, the better story is that you go to him. Recognize that his behavior is not a reflection of who he is but just of how he feels. Consider doing what Allen's parents did and offering him some options that are workable for him. If we do more of that, we will see far fewer college-aged young men on my therapy couch. That's definitely a better story.

Part Three

The Gaps

The Emotional Intelligence Gap

We raise our girls differently than we raise our boys. This may seem obvious, but it's important to point out that this remains the case, even as many of us work to bridge that gap. Far too often, we play to stereotypes, raising our girls to be pretty in pink, soft and gentle and demure. Our boys, on the other hand, we raise to be physical, powerful, rough-and-tumble, and unemotional. This was true several generations ago, and nearly every clinician and researcher I know would agree that this dynamic has not changed enough over the years.

One element of raising children we don't often think about is the development of emotional intelligence. The vast majority of parents remain sold on a wildly narrow definition of success, one in which grade point averages, standardized test scores, and the extensive extracurricular activities hold the key to entry into elite colleges, or at least the best possible institutions of higher learning. Grade portals, the growing ACT and SAT tutoring networks, and the new breed of college admissions books and online parent groups, as well as the *US News & World Report* collegiate rankings all create a huge push toward this type of objectively measurable accomplishment. We are further sold on the idea that said college admissions make for a happy, satisfying life, the kind of life pretty much every parent I have ever met proclaims they want beyond anything else for their children.

But I have spoken to very large groups of parents and counseled thousands of others, and when asked what qualities they hope to develop in their children, their answers are strikingly similar. Parents want their kids to grow up to be kind, thoughtful, independent, confident, and compassionate. We can be pretty easily thrown off from focusing on these qualities when we have access to grade portals and other ways of tracking our kids' grades and progress. We may fear our son lacks a needed competitive edge when he is falling behind someone else in a class, or is less involved in extracurricular activities, doesn't make the play, or sits on the bench, And this may cause our working definition of success to shift.

But to help you return your focus to those core qualities, development of emotional intelligence in your kids drives more success in all of those other areas as well. Some school districts across the country have adopted social emotional learning (SEL) programs because of the massive contributions they make to success. As a brief primer, emotional intelligence is in essence the ability to identify and manage your own emotions and to understand and empathize with the emotions of those around you. We are naturally drawn to emotionally intelligent people. We hire them more frequently, their relationships are more satisfying and longer lasting, and they are happier, and by almost any measure, more successful.

There is another fundamental component of emotional intelligence that we need to stress here, one that girls tend to manifest and boys tend to lack. We raise our boys to be independent in nearly every way: financially, socially, and emotionally. We expect our boys to be self-reliant—this is in part where we feel their strength is. Work independently, as if in a silo, and nobody else can take credit for your accomplishments. This is the traditional male way. But it also deprives us of certain opportunities for synergy in life, and is typically joyless in the end.

We teach our girls, on the other hand, to be cooperative and interdependent with one another. That is not to say we want them to be codependent, a dysfunction in which others are required to fulfill the vast majority of your emotional needs, and vice versa. This dynamic is also toxic and unhealthy, and it all but dooms a mutually satisfying relationship.

Give this a moment's thought. We want our boys to be as interdependent as our girls. We want them to work in collaboration with each other both on the job and in their private lives. We want our boys and young men to experience all the synergy, joy, and sense of connection enjoyed by our girls and young women.

Emotional intelligence is also a set of characteristics most often found in girls and women, and far less frequently in men. What I love about this group of qualities is that they are not set in stone; they are malleable. So, we can teach our boys to be emotionally intelligent; in fact, it is imperative that we do so.

Expert Tip: Building More Emotional Intelligence in Our Boys

As parents and other caring adults in the lives of young people, we often forget what it is we want for them. Most parents tell me they want their children to thrive and be happy, to do work that they love, to build and nourish deep and caring relationships, and to become good, caring, empathic people. But there is a din of books and honor roll bumper stickers and conventional goals that don't support this thinking at all. More and more, our kids are aware of the dissonant messages they are receiving from us:

- "Be happy, but be successful."
- "Stay up and do homework, but remember that self-care is crucial."
- "Creativity is important, but you really need to get some practice SAT tests in before Saturday."

In the midst of all this noise, we also forget what really drives success. When Daniel Goleman wrote *Emotional Intelligence* decades ago, his research discovered that, while knowing your stuff and having the ability to do the job well are important, these traits account for only about 10 to 15 percent of success. The other 85 percent is derived from something we call emotional intelligence: the ability to know and understand our own emotions and have some comprehension of the emotions of those around us.

Of course, we instinctively know our performance at work is going to thrive when we have the ability to read the emotions in any room. Emotional intelligence drives success not only in work, but as you might guess, in all of our other relationships as well. Marriage and other intimate relationships thrive with emotional understanding, as do friendships and connections between parents and children.

Now, here's the problem. From the youngest ages, we teach our girls to be empathic and caring and kind. We teach them emotional intelligence throughout their entire upbringing. And as they grow up, they begin to reap the benefits of this set of skills early. Again, emotional intelligence drives success. So it should come as no surprise that more young women are now enrolled in colleges and universities and law schools than young men, and that more women are entering the work force than ever before. Overall, it would be difficult to argue against the reality that not only are women breaking glass ceilings, but despite a ridiculously large continuing wage gap, they are being promoted to leadership positions and finding success as entrepreneurs at a rapidly increasing pace.

Some may see this as the sweep of history righting the wrongs of eons of unfairness, and that's probably true to some extent. I see this as a recognition in the marketplace of a previously undervalued and underutilized set of skills. I suspect that this trend will continue well into the future as women and the marketplace recognize the power and strength that lies not only in raw intelligence, but in the empathy and justice and synergy that are part of emotional intelligence.

And if we're being honest, we don't teach our boys to be emotionally intelligent. We teach them to be physically strong and competitive. But we wholly fail them in what are often deemed (erroneously, in my opinion) the "soft skills" of emotional intelligence.

But again, emotional intelligence can improve. If we model emotional intelligence for our boys, and in particular if fathers model these qualities for their sons, they will pick up on the cue that it's okay to tap into these skills and put them to use. So this is a call for parents, especially fathers, to talk with their boys about their feelings and the feelings of those around them. It can be an odd shift, but I've seen it happen in many of my client families, every one of which is better for it.

There is some good news woven in here for this current generation of young people. The emotional intelligence gaps between boys and girls, and between young men and young women, are beginning to close. Men are increasingly empathetic to the plight of others, including friends, family, and classmates, as well as those suffering around the planet. In fact, both boys and girls are ever more aware of all of the suffering across the planet at strikingly young ages. There is not a twelve-year-old in America unaware of the war in the Ukraine, or the severity of the climate crisis, or children starving halfway across the planet. They have ready access to this knowledge in the palm of their hand. We just need to provide our boys with a little push in the form of positive examples and permission to close this gap entirely. Empathy and compassion are there. They just need encouragement to express these feelings.

The Loneliness Gap

"I am so f-ing lonely. I honestly think most guys are.
And it's something none of us talk about."

—*Jason, sixteen*

Jason initially came into my office almost by accident. He had been suffering a difficult semester, and his mom asked him, just once, whether he was okay. He said he didn't think he was. He said he thought he might be depressed, but he wasn't sure. Within a few weeks of starting therapy, he talked about how very lonely he is. Curiously, he has people he sees and talks to. There are a few guys he plays video games with. But all of their contact feels kind of empty to him. Jason is a deep and thoughtful guy, and he's looking for something more out of his connections in relationships. He tells me that he knows other guys who are looking for the same. But somehow, nobody is "man enough" to admit this to other guys. He thinks it's because of this that he and all his other friends just wallow in loneliness.

Jason is of course not alone. I have heard this sentiment from so many boys over the years, especially over the past few years. Our boys and young men want deep and meaningful connections. But as Jason has pointed out many times, they weren't raised to foster those connections. He has told me many times in gut-wrenching detail that he believes he and all the guys he knows have the ability to connect. He doesn't think that boys lack this capacity. He just doesn't think they're allowed to feel, express, and connect the way girls are encouraged to do. This leaves them lonely, and Jason will tell you that loneliness is a dark and sometimes desperate place. When I told him I was writing this book, he asked me to punctuate the loneliness factor. He doesn't think his parents understand it. He knows his friends probably do, but they aren't saying anything. And he admitted that he was reluctant to talk with me about it.

"It's not a really strong position to come from, is it? Seriously, I think most guys would overtly say that talking about loneliness is for wusses."

But he and I both know that it's not.

In effect, we really need to address this loneliness issue with our boys. I think that most of us can safely assume that our boys are lonely at least some of the time. This is true despite the fact that many of them are immersed in groups of friends a lot of the time. If those friends are not connecting on a deeper level, then as Jason suggests, any guy can be lonely in a crowd.

Incidentally, Jason also thinks his dad is a lonely man. He thinks that males are basically lonely. A lot of the young men I work with would agree with Jason on this point. They envy peers with deep connections.

And oddly, sometimes for boys and men, these connections tend to come in the wake of either tragedy, crisis, or some other difficulty. I recently worked with some young men, college students, who had lost a close friend to suicide. In the wake of the tragedy, they found deeper connections with one another. One young man told me that doing so was imperative. "We cannot lose another guy because he feels alone."

Young men in recovery for alcohol and drug addiction also may have the opportunity to connect in a deeper and more meaningful way. I can see hope bubble up in my newly sober, young, male clients. It's remarkable, but not surprising.

I grew up in a sober house. I was born on the third anniversary of
my dad's sobriety. Every Thursday evening when I was growing up,
a group of twenty-five to thirty men would come to our house. My
brother and I would make two giant urns of coffee for them. And they
would sit for a couple of hours in our basement, where they would talk,
laugh, share their stories, and connect.

I can recall overtly violating the AA code when I was a kid by sitting
on the staircase, listening to these men. In retrospect, they modeled
for me a way to connect man-to-man. This proved to be essential in
driving my connections with my own male friends later in life.

So for certain categories of young men, including those going through
a crisis or significant change, connections are possible, necessary, and
possibly even lifesaving.

But we have to attend to all of our boys and young men, not just those
going through a crisis. So please, do not assume that your guy is not
lonely. In all likelihood, at least some of the time he is.

Expert Tip: Extinguishing the Loneliness

We need to talk directly with our boys about loneliness and
connection. Jason and some other young men have suggested that a
lot of guys may not know the degree to which they feel lonely. Lacking
emotional language, they just might think they feel bad, or sad. They
may also be frustrated with themselves for feeling that way.

We need to give our boys permission to feel whatever it is they feel,
authentically and openly. So talk to him about how you felt when you
were his age. Talking about times when you were lonely gives him
permission to talk about his loneliness without guilt or shame.

One remarkable thing about this is that once lonely young men start connecting with one another, it tends to have a ripple effect. A group of college sophomores losing a friend will undoubtedly foster stronger connections with one another. But they'll also connect more openly with other guys. Their conversations will become deeper and richer. Their connections will strengthen. And when times get tough, they will find that they really have each other to lean on. This is a very big deal.

The Hopelessness Gap

I suggested in the introduction that in my experience, the girls in my practice possess the facility to find hope through the darkest of times. They can reframe depression and sadness as important emotions to experience in their lives, while realizing that any happiness they enjoy shines brightly in contrast to some of these darker feelings. They can navigate the emotional process of counseling over the course of an hour, and they nearly always walk out of the room feeling more positive and hopeful than they did when they arrived. Hopelessness is not the center of their emotional universe for very long.

Boys and young men, on the other hand, tend to lack this capacity. So if they are among those who struggle to get out of their bedrooms or basements, who have a difficult time engaging socially or academically or athletically, an undercurrent of hopelessness may be what's holding them in place. Expressing anger toward them or disappointment in them will undoubtedly prove useless, as will punishments and consequences. Boys in these situations already feel all of this anger and disappointment toward themselves. And hopelessness arises when they feel as if they lack the capacity to move beyond these feelings.

The future either looks bleak to these young men, or they have difficulty envisioning a future for themselves at all. So many boys and young men say they cannot envision a happy future for themselves, and many of them are looking to us, the adults who surround them, to provide models of hope for a happy, healthy, relationship-rich, successful future. But they pay attention to what we do as well as what we say. Far too many young men clearly do not want the lives their parents have because their parents seem markedly unhappy or overtly express their discontent with their lives.

There are other reasons young men are not drawn to adulting. Not only do the activities of work and bill paying lack appeal for them, but they see no joy in the adults in their lives. It simply is not effectively demonstrated in ways they can understand.

Further, they read enough to realize that they may not be in a position to afford a successful future for themselves, financially or otherwise. Nothing about being an adult holds appeal, so they quite literally disappear in order to avoid this reality. It is important to note that this disappearing act is far more coping than cowardice.

Expert Tip: Reframing Negative Experiences to Create Hope

So many of our boys feel a strong degree of hopelessness about the future. Our instincts as parents are sometimes to try to talk them down from this—to encourage them to envision a bright and happy future. This can be a frustrating exercise, and it's typically unsuccessful. Your guy is more likely to feel as if you just don't understand than he is to think you're trying to help, despite your best efforts here.

Sometimes the way to create hope about the future is to help our boys reframe their past. I work with a lot of teenage boys who feel as if the world is against them. Their hopelessness is often engendered by experience, but that experience is often perceived through a wildly negative lens.

So, I typically ask what they mean when they say they feel hopeless. Sometimes they'll reference a girl who broke up with them. Sometimes they'll talk about a class in which they didn't do well, or parents who are grounding them for some infraction or another. Just as often, we look back at situations in which my clients have had some degree of agency. They may have come home too late, for instance, and that is the reason why they are grounded.

When we look back in this way, we always find something useful, for instance, some degree of possible agency on the part of the boy, or that the event was just a random, isolated incident. Once we do, we can reframe those experiences: "Okay, that is a negative thing that did happen to you, or that you caused to happen. Now tell me something positive that's happened as well." Or, "Is there something different that you could've done to avoid that situation?"

If we can loosen a teenage boy's negative thinking about his past, we create the opportunity for him to gain insight and place a brighter lens on the future. This is a super effective tool, and it's way easier than merely trying to talk them into looking differently at the future.

Sidebar: The Dark Side of the College Admissions Business

You may have noticed in recent years that countless bestselling books have been published suggesting the best ways to gain admission into the most desirable colleges, even if the college admissions sites suggest they may be out of your child's reach. It is no coincidence that these books have arrived in the wake of the notorious college admissions scandal in which a couple of Hollywood celebrity families were caught cheating the system. They did so by lying about their children's accomplishments and/or by offering unusually high sums of endowment donations in quid pro quo agreements; yet in the end, these parents were exposed as entitled cheats.

Recognizing the market for short cuts to getting into better colleges, a spate of wildly popular books for parents have come out, including *Who Gets in and Why, The Truth about College Admission, Colleges that Change Lives,* and *The Price You Pay for College,* among many others. The idea that young people, including young men, get from the quantity of such titles showing up in their homes is that their parents value achievement above all else. Now, I fully recognize that this may not be the motivation of either the authors nor of most parents, but young people tell me that the presence of these books ramps up pressure in an already anxiety-ridden and pressured area of their lives. This does not draw young people to the process of filling out applications and visiting campuses and getting excited about the four years to come; instead, these kids feel even more overwhelmed.

Before you order any of these books or even check any grade point averages, sit down with your son, or your daughter for that matter, when they are a sophomore or junior in high school. Ask them their thoughts about the future, but in an open, playful way. Allow them space to muse—to dream a bit about their future. After all, they have far less time in their lives to be idealistic about their futures than we did. Ask your son, "What would you want to do if you could do absolutely anything, even if it sounds ridiculous?" I have watched young people find their footing with that question alone, driven by the permission to play with the idea of a limitless future. Let them play with it, allowing them to brainstorm and toss ideas around without any weight attached to them. Eventually, you'll find a bit of magic strikes them, a lightning bolt that might not lead them in a linear direction yet provides initial clues to guide them toward the future they haven't yet conceptualized—a future they don't even yet know they yearn for.

The Opting Out Gap

In my years of working with teenage boys, I have observed a marked increase in those experiencing the opting out gap, which is closely related to the joylessness gap. Due to all of the negative influences and stressors they experience, I find that many of the boys and young men I work with opt out of their lives. They quit the sport, put down the instrument, break up with their girlfriend, divest themselves of their schoolwork. It's an alarming trend that is far, far more common in boys than girls, and one that has clearly exploded in magnitude since the onset of the COVID-19 pandemic, perhaps in part because opting out became not just a possibility but an actual mandate for safety.

So, I find myself working with many boys and young men who rarely if ever leave the house. They often vape nicotine and smoke pot, some of them throughout the day and night. They are bedroom or basement dwellers, alone the vast majority of the time, playing video games, scrolling through social media, watching way too much pornography, and listening to the Voices. They are resistant to movement of any kind, from chores to homework, from going to bed at night to waking up in the morning, sometimes even skipping family meals. Failing classes and missing school doesn't seem to motivate them. In fact, nothing does. For parents, this situation quickly shifts from perplexing to frustrating to downright frightening.

Here's the key, and I want you to read this twice. It's not the behavior but what lies behind the behavior that matters. Your son is not opting out of his life because he's lazy. He's not opting out because he doesn't care. He's not opting out to challenge your parenting ability.

And please keep in mind that your job is not to "force remedy" the behavior. Don't get me wrong. You may very well have the power and leverage to do that. But if you take away the car, the phone, or the allowance, you may very well change his behavior for a time. He may sign up for a sport or a club. He may get a job. He may do some homework in your presence—for a while.

But here's the reality, and it's a critical one: If you don't help your guy identify what drives his actions or his inaction, you're not really contributing to any lasting change, nor are you moving him in the direction of a positive, collaborative relationship with you. And he needs your help to begin to understand his own motivations. In all likelihood, he is feeling enough confusion and hopelessness that he may not want to tell you about it, but he needs you to help identify the most important thing: the *why*. Because I can assure you, he has precious little insight into his opting out. It likely scares him as well. He doesn't know why.

So, sit down and talk to him about how he feels about himself, his world, and his future. Be prepared, as I have had to be countless times, for the answers to be deeper, more thoughtful, and far more insightful than you expect. They also may be darker and less hopeful than you'd wish for your guy. An awful lot of parents believe their boys are not thinking—or not thinking enough—and that's the cause of the majority of their difficulties.

But the reality is quite the opposite. Your guys think all the time. It's all they do. They think about the world and their place in it. They fear they may not have a place in it. They think about whether they are worthy or worthwhile. They judge themselves for their selfishness (despite the fact that a large degree of self-centered thinking is requisite in order to navigate adolescence successfully). They know they're not doing enough, but they're either not sure what to do, or how to find the motivation to do it, or both.

All of this leaves them feeling frightened and alone. And in my experience, every one of these opting out young men is deeply anxious, and that anxiety can drive a young man into a pretty profound depression. All the porn and smoking and scrolling is simply weak medicine when it's up against such powerful internal suffering.

For better or for worse, this reality presents a massive parenting opportunity for you. If you can set aside your ego and your fears and judgments about his life, you can help him find his worth, his voice, and the building blocks of his purpose.

So, if you are involved with a teenage boy or young adult man who is opting out and at his worst, I strongly urge you to take rapid steps to reconfigure your approach. For he does not need your judgment or redirection. He knows. He does not need your lectures either. He knows them as well. Instead, show him your unconditional support, your love, your *gentleness*.

Recognize that this behavior is a signal of a difficult time for him, a time of pain and tough choices, a time in which he's trying to determine the nature of masculinity, be it toxic or divine, and where he belongs in that space. He needs love and acceptance. He is not his behavior—he is bigger and deeper than that. You may be frustrated with him because while you know this, he isn't showing it. But keep in mind that he's not withholding what you are hoping for on purpose. He just hasn't figured it out yet.

Remember that what he needs from you in the process of figuring it out is your support. Too often, parents panic in a moment, a week, or a month of opting out by their son. And I get it. Watching your child opt out while feeling powerless on the sidelines is awful. But if you keep the idea of *process* in mind, you'll find some space to breathe, and you will make better decisions as a parent.

With that in mind, the first decision you'll want to make is not to manage his behavior, but to begin a gentle discussion about the nature of the opting out. Keep in mind that fear and anxiety lie in the background of this behavior, and engaging with him while he's in their grip requires your compassion and care. He needs to know that you are fully available to him to talk through any and all elements of that fear. It will, in all likelihood, take some time for him to open up to you, but that time is a precious investment in the well-being of your son.

Then, provide him with some sense of hope. Muse with him about his future since he may be feeling very little hope in that regard. Get him to open up, and believe me, behavior change will follow. But bear in mind that opting out creates a powerful draw. It's easy to stay in that space. It's comfortable, even if it does nothing to change the anxiety he feels out in the world. He needs your assistance in defining himself and his place in the world before he'll be able to step back in.

Your job is to listen and to help him find the support and resources to do so. Of course, consult a clinical psychologist familiar with this phenomenon if necessary. If your guy is opting out, I'm virtually certain you'll need that outside help. It's an important part of good parenting.

The Joylessness Gap

The lives of our kids are far too serious and adult-like at ever-younger ages. As I write this, I have just wrapped up a live interview on the radio. I was a guest on a radio show talking about a mass school shooting that had taken place in Nashville just an hour or two earlier. My Facebook memories this morning showed that I was on the same program exactly a year ago, talking about another mass shooting in another school in another state. During a therapy session, I received three text messages from children who were in school at the time, alerting me of the day's attack. A potential school shooter is on the minds of our kids. The thought is second nature to them. It is ordinary:

"You can't tell me, Duffy, that it's not going to happen at my school. You can't. Because you know it totally could."

I had no reasonable response to that one. It was simply true.

At the same time, I'm working with a high school junior thinking about colleges. He has attained near perfect grades throughout high school, save for a single C in one semester in math his freshman year. As he attempts to gain admission to some elite schools, despite multiple and varied extracurricular activities, he fears he may have blown his chances with that one subpar grade a couple of years ago. He's consumed by this anxiety, and I cannot in good faith tell him that he is wrong. Further, this "deal-breaker" concern has been on his mind since he received that report card.

At fourteen years old.

Do you remember these types of concerns and anxieties when you were a teenager? Neither do I. Because as one of my young teenage clients accurately pointed out, we were never teenagers as they are. We never experienced the teenage world, stress and anxiety and all, the way today's teens do.

And there are distinct differences in the ways girls and boys navigate these stressors.

Stand outside a typical high school after the final bell rings on any given day, especially a Friday, when all the students are primed and excited for the weekend. Watch the girls. They are hugging and laughing and talking and planning. Their joy is barely contained. You'll catch a similar scene, by the way, on any given morning before the first bell rings. These girls, I'll remind you, have a lot on their minds. Some are depressed or anxious. Others are experiencing self-loathing to the point of self-harm, and some suffer with eating disorders or other emotional issues. They are far from immune from life's stresses.

Yet still, there is space in their lives and in their everyday for joy.

Our boys do not on the whole have the ability to share joy like the girls. Save for the deadly drone of video games, boys are done playing at younger and younger ages. Watch them during their free time before and after school, and you'll see a very different story unfold. In fact, these are the most highly visible moments of the day for teenagers, the brief breaks when they get to spend the most unprogrammed time together. So, if they want to put forth a certain image to their peers, these are prime opportunities to do so. Boys are often together, but bear with them a façade, a degree of masculinity and cool that doesn't allow them the freedom to let their guard down. Many are trying to maintain or achieve "alpha male" status with their peers—to be ringleaders for their crew, however large, of male followers. This is an enviable position in that these boys carry an awful lot of social cachet. Other boys tell me they navigate the hallways silent and alone, hoping to stay off the radar of their peers. A few do this to evade bullies, without a doubt. The majority, however, feel a degree of self-consciousness that drives enough social anxiety and potential self-doubt that they choose solitude very deliberately over connection— since trying to connect might lead to humiliation.

This differential between boys and girls is one we typically fail to note, but it carries significant consequences for both. Girls let out some of their anxiety during these crucial moments of the day (and we have now learned during the pandemic just how crucial those brief times are). They connect and create and strengthen bonds with one another in these moments, and for them, it requires only moments. They get fully out of their heads, play, hug, and experience joy.

Boys, on the other hand, hold their social positions. They maintain their personas as jocks, or academics, or just cool. They do not allow themselves to let their guard down to play and connect, because if they do, they risk revealing something that is actually more real than the façade, their true nature. They can calculate unconsciously how easily they can slide down the social ladder, or the masculinity ladder. Few boys are willing to take such risks. For girls, on the other hand, play in these arenas may actually increase the goodwill they carry with their friends and peers.

In order to close this gap, we've got to create circumstances under which boys and girls both feel free to drop the façade and play.

Expert Tip: Extracurricular Activity

I have noticed one distinct exception to the rule concerning boys and joy. Boys who are active and involved in sports, plays, groups, bands, clubs, and so on often play and experience the joy that is otherwise seemingly unavailable to them.

When he was in high school, my son was a swimmer and water polo player. My wife Julie and I were in the stands before warm-ups preceding a polo game one day, and she called me over to watch the team. These teenage boys were transformed, playing joyfully and without self-consciousness, pushing each other into the pool, splashing, and throwing the ball—things one might picture much younger boys doing. This opportunity for regression to an earlier time—and to pure joy—is a rarity for our boys.

The benefits of joy for our boys are immeasurable. When they're playing and joyful, all the stressors that bring about depression, isolation, anxiety, and loneliness fall away. The space provides sanctuary from the stressors that show up within textbooks as well as on screens, both in online headlines and through social media notifications. They need this break from the space between childhood and adulthood to get out of their anxious heads and be kids, fully and joyfully. It may seem like folly or an unnecessary indulgence, but this time is reenergizing and reinvigorating for our boys. They feel a sense of connection and fun and joy that they may not encounter again for the remainder of the day.

And to be clear, this joy is not reserved for the pool or playing field. Boys involved in all sorts of activities play in the margins, between the openings and closings, behind the curtain, and on the court. So, I strongly urge you to play the parent card here. Make participation in at least one extracurricular activity mandatory. Once your guy is a teenager, you will not have many opportunities—your deck holds increasingly fewer parent cards as your sons get older. But trust me, this is one card worth playing.

If your boys are not the type to be joiners or are not otherwise involved in extracurriculars, then I would encourage parents, caretakers, and siblings to press them to play at home. Boys are at their best, emotionally and otherwise, when they are physical at least part of every day. So, wrestle playfully with your boys. Make up ridiculous games.

I am not the perfect parent by any means, but my son and I made up a game in which we left a closet door ajar and took shots into the closet with everything from bottle caps to rolled up socks. We would play for a ridiculous amount of time—and this brought him joy, and a degree of goofiness he would not otherwise have experienced. Oh, I also loved it. Don't let the kids experience all the joy. If you do this right, there will be plenty to go around. Not that another benefit is necessary, but this type of play in the family increases your balance in the emotional bank account with your son, which builds your leverage with him when you really need him to hear you.

Case Study: The Taylor Swift Effect

When we talk about joy and playfulness, music often comes to mind for me. I love it when parents and their kids share music together, for a number of reasons. First, music can provide a shared vocabulary between the generations that can help bridge the gap in other areas as well. Music draws out emotion from within us, and sharing music is among the most intimate activities that parents can share with their kids, if they are willing to.

That said, I've worked with many parents who didn't like, or believed that they would not like, the music their kids listen to. When I can get parents to open their minds, this is often untrue. They usually find that music is more of a connector between them and their kids than it is a divider.

Taylor Swift was recently here in Chicago for her Eras tour. My office is about a mile from the venue. One night, she was going to be giving a concert. Over the course of that day and into the evening, I could see groups of girls and their mothers all decked out in their Swiftie finest, laughing and singing and playing and dancing in the streets of the city. It was a beautiful, colorful, explosion of joy that went on for hours. I love seeing moms with their daughters sharing an experience that I suspect none of them will ever forget. But if you think about it for a moment, there are few corresponding activities that connect fathers and their sons through joy. Occasionally, I will work with a father and son who are able to connect through music. Some will connect through sports, rooting together for their favorite teams. But these connections don't share the frenetic level of joy that I saw in moms and daughters the day of the Taylor Swift concert. Boys and their dads don't dance together. They may laugh together, but it's usually muted, brief, and decidedly "masculine."

So, I would encourage you to get creative in finding ways to share joyful moments like these with your boys. Sharing those times creates those beautiful memories to be sure. But they also deepen the connection between parent and child. They organically grow the balance in the emotional bank account between the generations as well. They create more intimate modes of communication, allowing for more openness and vulnerability. None of this should be underrated. These shared moments pay off in parenting now and make connections between generations that will last lifetimes. I love everything about this. Find this space with your boys. They need you there.

The Post-Pandemic Gap

I work with Tim, a twenty-year-old young man who was in high school throughout the pandemic. Before the pandemic started, when he was a sophomore, Tim was suffering from some school related and social anxiety. By the end of his sophomore year, the pandemic was already a couple of months old. And in virtual sessions with me, Tim was noting that that his anxiety had largely abated. He was actually feeling far better.

This was neither an uncommon nor a surprising result. Many of the anxious kids I worked with, both male and female, felt some degree of relief when not only were they quarantining at home, but everyone was. There was no face-to-face social interaction to be anxious about, there was no FOMO since there was nothing to miss out on, and most coursework was makeshift and far easier than it had been in person. Tim would joke that the pandemic was perfect for him.

He spent an awful lot of the next year in his bedroom. He by and large went to school in his bedroom. He played video games in the bedroom. He even went to therapy there, sometimes while in bed. And Tim's level of anxiety was pretty low during this period of time.

Tim fared pretty well emotionally through his junior year as well, with a lot of schoolwork still virtual, or else in classrooms that were only partially full, and with makeshift lunch and gym periods. He wasn't going out much at all, but neither was anybody else. He told me he felt safer being by himself than surrounded by others.

By his senior year, the school schedule—and a lot of youth social calendars—were heading back to normal. And in that same period, Tim's anxiety began to spike once again. He had an exceptionally difficult time just getting up and going to school. His anxiety crept into depression, and he became more inert and homebound than he had been during the pandemic.

And this makes some sense. For a lot of kids, reacclimating to being in school and with their peers required a degree of daily familiarization that may need to be reestablished. They weren't used to the academic and social stressors and hadn't been for some time.

And herein lies a critical difference I've noted between Tim and the boys I've worked with on the one hand and the girls I've worked with on the other. The girls I was working with bounced back from the pandemic pretty readily. They recouped their social connections and reengaged with school and extracurricular activities. This was true even for some girls I worked with who were suffering from anxiety, depression, and other emotional difficulties. I was impressed and surprised at the resilience of a lot of these girls and young women.

But the young men I've worked with since the pandemic haven't bounced back to that same extent. I find that this gender difference is due in large part to a lack of resilience, or perhaps to boys perceiving themselves as lacking in resilience. Girls and young women view themselves as resilient more so than boys, so they tend to feel some sense of assurance that they can navigate difficult times and unpredictable situations safely and effectively. They know they have tools to get through tough times and often leverage their relationships to do so. They talk to other people in their lives, including parents, friends, and other trusted adults, to help them problem-solve and manage their emotions in tough times.

Boys, on the other hand, may possess just as high potential to be resilient. But because of their outdated definition of masculinity, they are more likely to try and work through difficulties on their own. As a result, they often avoid challenges because they fear they may not be able to manage them independently, leading to a sense of failure as a person if they don't prove themselves entirely capable in trying circumstances. So while myriad girls have proven themselves to themselves, many of our boys have not ever challenged themselves in this way. This can result in avoidance, a drop in self-esteem, and a feeling that they may not be particularly capable when dealing with hardship. I would not have written a book about boys five years ago, but seeing the difference in the way they've bounced back—or have not—since the pandemic peaked and in-person schooling resumed has been impossible not to notice.

I actually think our boys were already struggling more—in silence— before the pandemic. Like Tim, many of them settled into the pandemic, their anxieties soothed by the lack of exposure to almost any stimuli outside of screens. Where our girls have been conditioned to manage their emotions and seek out connections and even help when they need it, our boys have not been brought up that way.

So, once the odd comfort of the pandemic was gone, the emotional difficulties boys had been suffering became far more apparent. Because they have not been conditioned to understand and manage their own emotional lives, their emotional difficulties shifted from being latent to overtly obvious and apparent as the pandemic drew to an end.

For years, I've suggested the goals of parenting are competence and resilience. If our kids go out to college or whatever their next adventure is at seventeen, eighteen, or nineteen years old, we want them to know that they are competent. We want them to know that they are capable of taking on challenges and mastering things for themselves. We want them to know that they are able to seek help when they see the need.

We also want them to know that they are resilient, that they have the capacity to withstand and recover from challenges and difficulties in their lives. And many of our boys don't feel a sense of competence and resilience. Again, I don't think that that's because they are incapable or because they lack resilience. I just think they believe these things about themselves.

So, part of our job as their parents is to present them with stepwise challenges so that they can prove themselves capable, competent, smart, resourceful, and resilient. And as we've indicated, we need to teach them the emotional language to understand how they feel and how those around them feel, and an awareness of when seeking help becomes necessary. These are the tools we've been encouraging our girls to make use of forever. It's time to do the same for our boys.

The pandemic has shown us a lot of who we are as people. Overall, I think we learned that we are willing to do difficult things to make it through difficult times, and that we are willing to be supportive of one another. In an odd way, much of our collective reaction has proven hopeful to me. I think we rose to that occasion really well.

Post pandemic, I think we're learning some things too. And we would be remiss if we didn't attend to the way our boys are reacting to these transitions.

Case Study: School Refusal

"Every day, I go to bed, hoping I can do it. Hoping I don't let
my parents down or myself. And every morning, I get up so
bummed and discouraged. And I just can't make it out the
door. Sometimes, I can't even make it out of bed."

—Aaron, sixteen

A decade ago, I had not worked with a single teenager, male or female, who outright refused to go to school. In the years since, and particularly following the pandemic, I have worked with dozens. Not incidentally, they have all been boys. School refusal is a particularly distressing issue for parents. With each passing day of non-attendance, the situation slowly slips from something concerning to an outright crisis.

We find ourselves pleading and begging our guys to go to school. As bargaining chips, we find ourselves extending curfews, video games, screen time, and more. Yet the vast majority of parents I have worked with have found all of these interventions to be wholly ineffective. Post pandemic, this is becoming an increasingly serious issue because kids have formed a habit of not going to school, given that was the rule for so long. Now, we are looking at the first generation of kids for whom this feels like a viable long-term possibility. Overall, we inherently know it is very unhealthy, as well as so very difficult to undo once it's habitual.

And once again, we parents have had to focus on behavior here instead of the underlying emotion. It's another area where our boys overestimate the impact of their anxiety and other symptoms. They predetermine before ever walking into the therapy room that they are neither capable nor competent to manage their way through the school day. Even with the availability of school social workers and psychologists, they feel enfeebled and emasculated. Their inclination is to hide. More than once, I have worked with parents who throw in the towel and opt for alternative school settings or homeschooling for their school refusing boys. I totally get it, but I think by doing so, we're missing the most important point. Once again, we have to think about the why, and the why almost always lies more in the underlying emotion than the behavior.

So, if you are a parent with a teenage boy who cannot seem to make it to school, follow my lead. It took me a while to learn that this was not a behavioral issue, and that pressing and prodding wasn't going to solve this problem. Instead, I strongly urge you to soften your stance. Ask your son what is stopping him from going to school, why it seems difficult. Let him know you have total faith in him and remind him of the resources he has available.

Honestly, in my experience, even that will likely not be enough. School refusal is driven by a profound level of anxiety and lack of self-esteem. I have yet to encounter the young man who didn't need therapy in order to work his way out of such emotional difficulties. So if your son refuses to go to school, don't wait another day to reach out to a therapist who has experience with this behavioral response. There are a lot of us out there.

Once you've got this team behind you, you can assume your role as a supporter of your son, focusing far more on his strengths than his difficulties. In the end, this is what he most needs from you in these circumstances.

Sidebar: The COVID Class

"Everyone paid the price for COVID, no doubt.
But our class, we got screwed worse than anybody."

—*Jaime, twenty-one*

As suggested above, the COVID-19 pandemic wreaked havoc on our kids, especially our boys. But a few moms I've talked to have suggested that some classes were more affected by the pandemic than others. Think for a moment about the high school class of 2020, Jamie's class. This class missed out on a prom. They missed out on the expected ritual of graduation. Many missed out on final seasons with their teams and parent nights. Some missed out on potential championships. Some missed out on appearing in the final play of their high school acting careers, and even possibly of their lives.

Now, for those in Jamie's class who went to college, picture what that first semester on campus was like. On many campuses, students spent the first weeks or the first semester quarantined in their rooms with just a few people. They didn't have a club night on the quad to sign up for groups, sports, clubs, and plays they were interested in. There were no freshman initiation rites: no dances, no dorm parties, really not much of anything but sitting in their room, drinking or smoking. They took their classes online, so their ability to meet other anxious new freshmen was eliminated.

I had a long discussion with one mom about this, and we realized there's really nothing that can be done to mitigate these losses for these kids. But I think it's reasonable that we recognize what they've been through. If they're struggling in one way or another, I think it's important that we acknowledge that COVID served some role in their difficulties. We can afford them some degree of grace.

I think we owe that to this group.

Part Four

The Problems

The Porn Problem

I'm going to be honest with you here. I have a strong negative bias against pornography. My concern with porn is that it can function as a cultural toxin, evoking some of the worst, darkest instinctual reactions from us. I also resent the absolute availability of pornography to our kids and, in particular, to our boys. Because young boys hold access to porn in the palm of their hands virtually all the time. I work with boys who get lost in this world hour after hour, day after day. It distorts their feelings about women and sex, bodies and the way they look, and the way it should work when people physically interact. Far too often, the line between sex and violence is blurred.

Pornography robs our boys of the innocence of those initial murmurs of attraction in their minds and bodies. What I observe with the teenaged guys I work with who watch porn is that these boys aren't excited about girls (or other boys or others, depending on sexual preference). They are not excited by real-life human beings. They have been deprived of that compass of arousal that creates a mixture of excitement and anxiety about what to do next. This is such a fundamental and awesome part of the adolescent experience, and I resent porn for robbing our kids of these moments.

I've learned that so many of our boys have been watching porn since they were eight or nine years old, far too young for this innocent side of them to die. It's created a deep and real crisis of identity for boys. Teenage boys tell me that when they first look at porn, it is alarming and traumatic. Most recently, a boy referred to his early introduction to pornography as a violent assault on his mind.

But of course, in the same breath, porn is tantalizing. There's a natural draw to sex. But the sex our boys are witnessing is false, choreographed, and scripted. After hundreds or thousands of hours of viewing, boys become overly acclimated to sex, numb to it, desensitized to their own natural reactions. And porn also becomes the metric by which they measure themselves, as well as potential partners.

What a rip-off.

There is now an endless availability of pornographic material to our young people, the primary consumers of which are our boys and young men. As I've stated, I have worked with many of these guys over the course of the past several years. They watch porn—a lot of it. Some teenage boys have told me they'll watch for five or six hours some days. Many of them begin watching pornography, which they often stumble upon while scrolling, as early as eight or nine years old. And they never stop.

It is tough to blame them when you hear about the trajectories of their initial exposure to this material. They tend to either stumble upon a pornographic website, or are told by a friend (or the friend of a friend) that they need to check out PornHub or some other similar website. Such websites are now considered "pop porn," offering far lighter fare than that can be found in the grimiest corners of the dark web.

Naturally, with such ease of availability of porn, our boys are drawn to it. They're curious, and the very idea of it is tantalizing to them. We cannot blame them for these types of urges. For better or worse, an attraction to porn makes perfect sense given where teenage boys are developmentally. And frankly, I have some concerns about the boy— or girl for that matter—who has no interest in sex, sexuality, and these days, even porn. Whether we like it or not, this is their norm, and I don't see that reality shifting any time soon.

In contrast, consider the obstacles before a boy trying to get his hands on pornographic material just a few decades ago. He would have to gain the trust of an older brother with access, or a father or other male relative. The most exposure most boys could gain to the female form was in *Cosmopolitan* magazine or the Sears catalog. I know many readers long for the days when this was the extent of a parents' concern about porn and sex.

That said, boys now develop large swaths of their belief systems about girls and women, relationships, sex and sexuality, and masculinity and femininity based on their exposure to pornography. Porn violates a sacred, joyful area of their lives and hijacks their development in a number of arenas, leaving them stymied, paranoid, anxious, confused, and often traumatized. This is deeply troubling, especially because many of them feel porn is somehow a reflection of reality, or even of an ideal. They do not often consider the fact that they are watching actors playing out roles in productions that prey on the fantasies of their viewers in order to keep them hooked long enough to click to watch the next video. And the next. And the one after that.

We need to pause for a moment here and focus on what boys tell me they think and feel when first exposed to pornography.

First, I can tell you from experience that our boys take pornography both literally and seriously. That said, once they are with another girl or boy in a sexual way in real life, the situations tend not to evolve organically, but instead are tainted by what our boys *believe* should be happening based on what they've spent countless hours watching and studying.

The results tend to be an unhealthy jumble. Boys come into sexual situations with predetermined expectations of what's supposed to happen and how. Specifically, they feel they are supposed to perform in ways that mirror those of the actors they've been watching. And because almost every moment they've been watching is fictitious, their beliefs here are altogether unreasonable.

Further, boys and young men expect their partners, female, male, or other gendered, to respond to their prowess in ways that mirror what they've been watching. You can just sense how toxic and wildly unsatisfying, even traumatizing, this must be for both parties. It's heartbreaking that this part of their lives that should contain such beauty and connection instead becomes a source of anxiety and fear.

And please keep in mind that absolutely none of what these boys study in pornography before their early sexual encounters has anything to do with love, caring, gentleness, or depth of connection. Instead, they've learned that sex acts are rote and robotic, but they are also inclined to measure their own manliness on their ability to replicate the entirety of the scene. This drives an awful lot of undue anxiety in our boys and young men. We'll get back to that and discuss it further. First though, let's consider the impact pornography must have on the ways our boys are learning to think about girls and women. Women and girls are 100 percent objectified, without question. And for many boys deep into their porn-viewing careers, female human beings are also dehumanized pawns who exist to show evidence of pleasure not for their own sake, but only in service of the man they are with. What a dramatic step backward culturally. Still, I can assure you, I'm talking to boys, and this is a reality.

And when things in a real-life encounter do not go the way of porn scenes, boys and young men begin to resent girls and young women. Because young men's egos are so deeply involved, they sometimes entirely lose their compass of reason. By way of examples, I have heard the following comments about this phenomenon recently in my office:

- "If they're going to withhold like that, I have to assume women hate me. And honestly, that makes me hate them back."

- "I think this whole LGBTQ movement is basically about girls hating guys, period. They're trying to show us they don't need us."

- "How am I supposed to feel about girls who don't put out for me while other guys are scoring all the time? Am I not good enough? The whole thing pisses me off."

These feelings boys are developing around women are not incidental or fleeting but are a core part of the problems I hope to address. If from an early age boys feel this deep resentment of girls in one area, it tends to expand to others as well. And that resentment is supported mightily by the Voices that drive the attitudes of our young men.

As you can see, porn does not make young men feel powerful, sexually or otherwise, over women. Quite the contrary; most young men I've worked with have reported to me that they feel women hold all the power in this regard. This far too often leaves boys resentful of girls and men resentful of women. The Voices support and amplify these feelings of resentment, putting their feelings of sexual disempowerment and emasculation into words.

In fact, many studies over the past decade or so have reported that young people, and young men in particular, are having less sex than they have in decades. This should come as no surprise given that the performance bar they envision in their minds is truly ridiculous. Many boys tap out of sexual contact of any kind. Ten years ago, teenage boys were spending a lot of their therapy hours talking about girls with a sense of excitement and appropriate anxiety. Now, boys hardly talk about girls at all unless asked. And as a therapist, that breaks my heart. For the future of their relationships, it could indicate something far worse.

Sidebar: Porn as a Catalyst for Questioning Sexual Orientation?

The viewing of pornographic material by our young men is so common that, after a certain tipping point, it can even cause them to sincerely question their own sexuality. An astonishing number of sexually active boys and young men I have worked with over the past several years report to me that their sexual response is diminishing. They are less turned on by their partners than they feel they should be. And frankly, the more I hear about this phenomenon, the more it is clear this is a major and disturbing trend.

Though this may be an uncomfortable request, think about the potency of your body's sexual response when you were attracted to someone as a teenager or young adult. It was powerful and undeniable. And this is the normal, natural evolution of attraction. It's nothing to be ashamed of. Quite the contrary, it's among the greatest things about being young and in a state of heightened hormonal arousal—of unmistakably exciting attraction to another human being.

Now, consider the plight of boys and young men who have been desensitized by excessive exposure to porn. More than a dozen have reached out to me over the course of the past several years as porn has become ever more accessible, and their concerns stretch well beyond underperforming relative to their counterparts. Instead, many of these young men question their own sexuality.

- "I'm not that turned on by my girlfriend, Duffy. Do you think I might be gay?"
- "I find myself testing my physical reaction to attractive men. And I'm worried I may be homosexual or bisexual."

These concerns are arising with increasingly frequency in my practice. If these young men were truly on a quest to determine the nature of their sexuality, as so many young people are doing these days, I suppose I would be far less concerned for them. In fact, these confused young men are not against homosexuality. They just want to know— but because of the volume of porn they consume, their meter for gauging that is now poorly calibrated.

These young men are however straight. They are attracted to women and always have been. But their lack of a physical response to real-life partners brings up a burgeoning new emotional disorder many are already deeming HOCD: Homosexual Obsessive-Compulsive Disorder. This is not yet a diagnosable condition, but based on the boys I'm working with, it's just a matter of time before it's in the manual. It's an apt description of what these boys and men are going through, and for many of them, these thoughts do become obsessive and compulsive, and sometimes intrusive. In one session, we can talk it through, and it seems as if it's settled. But this concern is tenacious and tends to return over and over again. These thoughts infect many relationships that, in my estimation, could be quite healthy if the toxic impact of pornography did not affect the young men involved.

Expert Tip: The Porn Problem

In all likelihood, your teenage boy has watched countless hours of pornography in his lifetime. You may dread any talk of porn and sex with your son, but that cannot stop you from engaging with him on these topics. In fact, if yours is like so many of the families I have worked with over the past few years, you may be surprised to find that he is far more comfortable than you are when addressing these areas of life.

I do encourage you to approach your guy with care here. I'll remind you that what should be a beautiful, exciting, and tender area of his life may now in all likelihood be harsh and ugly and anxiety-provoking for him. You have an opportunity to reset all of that, but it requires you to put aside your discomfort. If it helps, tell him you're uncomfortable addressing this with him, but it's just too important to ignore. If this goes the way I've seen it in family sessions, he'll afford you some grace here for your discomfort. If you can inject a modicum of humor into that conversation, you'll move the discussion along that much faster.

Following are a few approaches I've seen work for parents in addressing the issue of porn with their boys. Some parents share their own experiences with pornography and the degree to which it distorted their views on sex and relationships, and what was required to recalibrate their thinking. This has proven to be a particularly effective approach because it puts parent and child in the same space and eliminates the majority of the potential shame for the son. It works particularly well if Dad, the parent your son most identifies with, is involved in the conversation.

Other parents have found success in talking with their sons about what watching porn is like for them, while overtly indicating that there is no penalty for answering and there are no incorrect answers. The more sheepish parents I've worked with have simply told their sons they are available to talk anytime about porn and sex. It's not necessarily my preferred method, but it's far better than ignoring the issue altogether.

The Body Image Problem

When we think about body image issues, the concerns of teenage girls often come to mind. And without a doubt, nearly every teenage girl and young woman I've worked with has suffered from significant concerns about their bodies. What's become more apparent recently is a steep increase in body image concerns among teenage boys.

Most boys today often experience conflicting feelings about what the ideal body type is. Some of the boys I've worked with are intent on becoming as muscular and "jacked" as possible. They'll go to the gym for a couple of hours every day, and they supplement their diets with protein powders, creatine, and sometimes steroids. Much like many of the girls I've worked with in the past, I find that these boys are never happy with their bodies, nor even approaching anything like a state of satisfaction with them. They can find flaws no one else would ever perceive. This often devolves to the dangerous point of dysmorphia, a preoccupation with perceived flaws only they can see that typically don't exist at all.

On the other side of the spectrum, there's a growing surge of boys attempting to create a waifishly thin frame. Diagnoses of eating disorders are rising quickly among the male population. I am currently working with several boys who are restricting, binging, and purging in order to manifest the tiniest body possible.

Talking to some of these teenage boys, I find that they come by their concerns quite honestly. Just as teenage girls have been for decades, these boys are now inundated with images of perfect male bodies. From their TikTok or Instagram feeds to the pornography they watch, many boys feel what one young man told me: "I just don't look right." The comparisons they make between their own bodies and these ideal images can be downright agonizing.

Some boys have shared with me that their body image issues are part of their confusion about masculinity in general. What is a man's body supposed to look like? How is my body supposed to feel?

For boys, their body image issues and the press toward creating a perfect body also involve their sense of agency. There are so many areas of their lives that they cannot control, so a lot of boys now recognize they can control what they consume, whether they work out or not, and what their body will look like. Managing this provides them with some sense of agency in a world that feels out of control at times.

What is certain is that we can no longer ignore the body image issues of our boys. We need to be thoughtful and clear about our messaging because it exerts a powerful influence on how they behave. I find it is useful when parents talk to their boys about being strong and healthy. As with any teenager, however, I see it is damaging when parents talk specifically about weight or body type with them. And sometimes, parents are far too cavalier with their words here. So I really want to caution you to be thoughtful.

In some circumstances, some of you may find you are a little out of your depth here. If you see wild fluctuations in your son's weight or body shape, or if he becomes secretive about his eating habits, I urge you to consult a specialist in teenage eating disorders, specifically someone who has experience with teenage boys.

And finally, I want you to keep the goal in mind here. We want our boys to feel good about themselves. We want them to feel strong, capable, and healthy.

The Weed Problem

*"Way more than half the guys I know smoke or vape weed
every single day. A lot of guys start first thing in the morning,
like, before their feet hit the floor. I don't know any girls who
smoke like that."*

—Alex, nineteen

Like Alex, I also know a lot of boys and young men who smoke with
that degree of frequency. I have not worked with one single girl or
young woman who smokes so much weed.

So, why is this a problem? Well, as indicated earlier, weed is a way for
our boys to officially opt out of any given day, week, month, or year
of their lives. They alter their state not to get high, but just to get by.
Weed is a survival mechanism for a lot of these boys. It doesn't really
do much to manage their stressors. Yet it does numb them to some
extent to the debilitating effects of those stressors.

But self-proclaimed "stoner" guys are not happy. Quite the contrary:
They are, to a boy, remarkably unhappy. This is why they smoke.
Weed provides a reprieve from their real-world cares. In the past
couple of weeks, teenage boys have described their weed habits to
me as "a vanishing act," "an induced coma," and "a total coping
mechanism" to combat and blur anxious and depressive thoughts.
All of that is to say that smoking marijuana is not fun for the majority
of our boys. It is in effect self-prescribed medicine for their ailing
psyches. As parents, it's really important that you recognize this
reality. Otherwise, you will find yourselves targeting the behavior
instead of the underlying problem. I've worked with too many parents

who have relied on drug testing and room searches, becoming de facto police officers in their own homes.

You may achieve compliance with a smoke-free, vape-free policy, but without addressing the underlying emotional issues, they will simply manifest elsewhere. Or, in many instances, what looks like compliance may not be compliance at all. Teenage boys have the internet at the ready. They can discover ways to beat drug tests. They can hide weed virtually anyplace. And vape pens are so miniscule they can hide them literally anywhere.

So, if your guy is smoking weed, I can assure you, he is not alone. He knows many, many other guys who smoke a lot as well. When we grew up, weed was pretty taboo for most of us. In my high school graduating class of a thousand, most of us can recall just a few names of people who smoked regularly. Smoking weed was considered "doing drugs." But that is no longer the case. These boys do not feel like they are doing drugs. Weed is far too common for them to feel that way. Boys who deal to one another also don't feel like they are drug dealers. They're just brokering a weed purchase for their friends. Seriously.

And I think we all know that marijuana is a very different drug than it once was. I read recently that in 1975, weed was thirty times less potent than it is today. So it's a far more powerful drug now, and it's legal in more and more parts of the country. This puts parents in a particularly difficult dilemma. I have moderated many debates between teenage boys and their parents about the utility of weed. Many boys are arguing for a medical marijuana card. They want to be able to get marijuana from a dispensary to medicate their depression, anxiety, or other maladies they might be suffering. This is a common occurrence. I don't think we're talking about it enough.

These boys press their parents, pointing out somewhat accurately that weed is a far less dangerous drug than alcohol, one which carries little to no taboo whatsoever. In fact, many fearful parents who are pushed into this corner by their sons in my office ask them if they would just drink alcohol and eliminate weed.

I totally understand this parental approach, as well as the fear and anxiety behind it. But we are missing the point here. It's important to note why our boys and young men are smoking. If we can address the why of it, then we can begin to mitigate the weed problem in their lives.

So you might be wondering what we're supposed to do about this weed problem. How do we address that why? Well, let's start by talking about what not to do. We can't ignore it, not anymore. Most boys smoke sometimes, and a lot of boys smoke all the time. Therefore, we have to talk to them about it.

And the conversation we have might be uncomfortable for us, because we are probably going to hear some dark thoughts—things we don't want them ever to think or feel. But once they open up and begin to talk about some of their darker feelings—the fact that they feel hopeless or lonely or unsure of what the future holds for them—once they talk through all of that, they can begin to heal. In my experience, once our boys begin to address their darker emotions, the light dawns fairly quickly. Emotional expression is, in my experience, the answer to the weed problem, as well as the solution to many of the other maladies our boys suffer. Keep in mind that difficult conversations often precede open emotional expression. So be prepared to have those hard talks. Hang in with him, and trust that it is a process, not one moment in time, that will bring good results and lasting benefits. I'm asking for some mighty parenting here, but you won't regret it.

Case Study: Vape Pens

Not long ago, I began working with a sixteen-year-old boy who I'll call Glen who started smoking weed when he was twelve. It was just experimental at first, of course. He knew one other guy his age whose big brother provided weed to him and his friend. Back then, they were smoking the flower itself. In the past thirty years or so, even cannabis herb has become far more heavily loaded with concentrated THC.

Then, when he was thirteen, a friend gave Glen his first vape pen. These are dangerous little things that dispense vapor containing between 30 and 70 percent THC. This young man became kind of a connoisseur of THC in general and vape pens in particular. He was concerned with the safety of my other clients, so he showed me what a "good vape" looks like and how it differs from a "bad vape." The difference was really alarming. And he wasn't wrong. An ER doctor I spoke with told me the same. He also told me that we don't know yet the repercussions of vaping THC, but he suspects they are decidedly not good.

Right around his sixteenth birthday, Glen was vaping first thing in the morning every day, before he even got out of bed. It was also the last thing he would do before he went to bed. Up to this point, he had convinced himself that he used THC just to numb out during the pandemic. He used it, he claimed, a lot like his phone or video games. He vaped all day long, every day. At some point, we agreed he had a problem.

He entered a rehab facility voluntarily to detox from marijuana. He left within thirty-six hours without completing his rehab. Two weeks later, his parents and I were able to get him back into that facility. A month later, he was no longer vaping. He decided never to use marijuana again.

He requested that I write about this here because the assumption held by his peers is that marijuana is safe and nonaddictive. He wanted me to relay his report that this is decidedly untrue. Glen wanted me to tell you that your kids can be addicted to marijuana, and in particular to the active ingredient, THC. He is certain he was addicted.

Glen asked me to be aware of this potential for addiction with my clients, and to share his story with them and their parents. He suspects, as I do, that a lot of boys who were not able to cope very well during the pandemic quietly, secretly, and unwittingly became addicted to THC.

The diagnostic manual for mental disorders is far behind the reality of my young client's life; while it lists criteria for addiction to a number of dangerous drugs, it sidesteps the potential for addiction to cannabis or THC, offering only Marijuana Use Disorder as a possible diagnosis.

So again, I do encourage you to talk to your boys about the use of weed. Cannabis is not what it used to be, and it is a dangerous place to hide, likely more dangerous than any of us knows. And as my client would tell you, it can be straight-up addictive.

Sidebar: Other Drugs

In my experience and that of my colleagues who work with boys and young men, marijuana is the drug of choice for more and more of our young guys. That does not, however, mean it's the only drug they're using or abusing. A lot of our guys drink to excess fairly frequently, but I haven't noticed that this has changed much over the course of the last few years. Binge drinking remains a fairly serious problem as well, especially in the unregulated atmosphere of a college campus. A lot of our guys are experimenting with other drugs as well. Hallucinogens like mushrooms and LSD are increasingly common, I find, though, to be fair, they tend to be used rather sparingly.

Since the arrival of vaping ten or twenty years ago, nicotine is now probably the most abused drug amongst our boys. Initially, boys think vapes (and all the apparatus that comes with them) are pretty cool. If you've ever seen one, they really are. You can see where a fourteen- or fifteen-year-old boy would be drawn to: the coil, the cartridge, and the sleek style of a vape pen. And these boys become experts at examining vapes. Further, cartridges can contain varying percentages of nicotine. Once they're using regularly, boys are often drawing serious quantities of nicotine into their bodies, often without thinking about it. Because vapes are nearly odorless and practically invisible, if a boy wants to hide his vaping, he can vape virtually anywhere and anytime. He can vape in class. He can vape in his room. He can vape in the shower.

So a lot of the boys and young men I work with are now quite addicted to nicotine. A friend of mine who is an ER doctor reached out to me about a year ago. He asked me if the boys I'm working with have been vaping, and I told him yes. He told me he's deeply concerned about the long-term effects of vaping on the lungs and cardiovascular systems of our guys. The "juice" inside a vape is sticky and numbing. This ER doc fears that this gunk adheres to the interior lining of the lungs. Long-term, he thinks we're going to see serious cardiovascular disease in our young people, especially young men.

I loathe these things for how cleverly designed they are. And they so readily drive our boys to addiction that it honestly infuriates me.

To double down on this issue, I should also note here that I think the top gateway drugs are actually marijuana and nicotine. With vaping, the delivery systems for the two can be quite similar. I rarely work with a young man who uses one and not the other. This is just another thing I need you to know.

Cocaine also seems to be coming back in vogue amongst our young guys too. It is not uncommon for teenage boys or young men to day drink, then do a line or two of cocaine in order to have the energy to go out and drink more. In the past couple of years, I've worked with more than a few young men who have made a habit of this. That's a significant concern to be sure. But I've also worked with a few young men who do cocaine nearly every day. Curiously, in my small sample group of clients in my practice, all of these regular cocaine users had been prescribed stimulants for ADHD when they were younger. I'm not sure there's causation there, but the correlation is a curious one.

We'd be remiss if we didn't address the abuse of prescription drugs here as well. Boys have told me stories about Ritalin and Adderall changing hands frequently. This can happen anytime, but it seems as if it's far more frequent around exam season. Boys use this stuff to focus, concentrate, and improve their performance. There is also a vast market for Xanax, Klonopin, Valium, and other benzodiazepines. I have worked with a handful of boys who have required hospitalization for benzodiazepine withdrawal without their ever having had a prescription for these medications.

Over the past five years or so, we've all heard a lot about fentanyl, a painkiller typically reserved for anesthesia and post-operative applications in hospitals. By now, however, we know that fentanyl is on the street. Somewhere up the chain, drug dealers lace other drugs with fentanyl in order to intensify the high. I suspect we have all read news stories and headlines where our young people, particularly our young men, accidentally overdose on some drug laced with fentanyl. Just among my own clients, I've seen young men who have inadvertently ingested fentanyl that a dealer had used to enhance the effects of marijuana, ostensibly to encourage buyers to come back frequently for more.

Case Study: A Cautionary Tale

I need to share with you a rather chilling story, one that I've seen repeated almost twenty times in the last six or seven years. I worked with a young man I'll call Jackson who went to visit his friends at a different university. He was not typically a weed smoker, but his friends were, so he decided to partake just this once. As it turns out, the marijuana he smoked that night was laced with fentanyl. He woke up the next morning convinced that there was something very, very wrong with his brain. To hear him tell it, he couldn't think straight. He felt odd and different and experienced a sense of depersonalization, as if his body and mind were not his own. He felt teary and emotionally out of control. He rushed home, and his parents were so alarmed at his story that they took him to an emergency room. The ER doctors were the ones who told him he'd used fentanyl, since he had no knowledge of it. They assured him he would feel better soon and sent him home.

Over the course of the next several weeks, he just felt worse. He could not stop thinking about how his mind wasn't working. Now this young man, a brilliant student, dropped out of school because he was certain he could not think straight. Before Jackson first landed in my office, he had spent three months at home—three solid months. He had gone out only to see his primary care doctor, who assured him he was fine physically and nothing was wrong. He pursued brain scans and an MRI, all confirming the same. He was actually disheartened to hear that there was nothing wrong with his brain. He was certain that the doctors had missed it. For surely, he wouldn't feel this way if he didn't have a brain tumor, or else an impending aneurysm or brain bleed. He honestly believed all of this. His anxiety around his neurological health was relentless.

It took several months of therapy and demonstrations of his intellectual acuity in the therapy room to prove to Jackson that he was actually okay. But more than a year later, his heightened vigilance and obsession around this still sometimes drives the perception of phantom symptoms. Even though he intellectually knows he's okay, his emotions still get the best of him, and he fears he is not.

I don't share this story as a scare tactic. But I've seen this phenomenon often enough to feel I need to bring it to your attention here. Whenever I work with a young man—or indeed with any young person—I always share the story. I want them to know what the risks are when they're smoking weed or taking some other drug.

I encourage you to do the same with your sons, and maybe with your daughters as well. The risk is real, and I suspect that if more of our kids know to keep an eye out for this phenomenon, it might be less likely to affect their lives in such a way. It might make them think twice before they use it in the first place. I've been lucky enough, I suppose, that I've never worked with anybody who has died by fentanyl poisoning. But I see headlines about young men dying that way nearly once a month. Because something so seemingly innocuous can lead to something so deadly, we can't dismiss it. We have to pay attention to what's happening and talk about it with our kids.

I feel I should offer one more thought here. Most kids who deal drugs of any kind today do not consider themselves drug dealers. A lot of kids don't even look at marijuana as a drug at all. Most would say it's just friends brokering for friends.

Just as often, however, our boys are buying drugs off of enticing menus on social media. You may have read that some parents have recently filed a suit against Snapchat to find a way to prevent kids from posting menus that their "clients" can order from online. I hope they're successful, but I doubt they will be. Kids are way savvier with social media than we are, and no doubt dealers will find a way to make their "products" available in this very efficient manner.

What I find parents don't want to believe is that dealers don't have to seek out buyers. Kids seek out dealers far more often. It is not unlikely that your son has bought drugs through a dealer on Snapchat or some other online medium. This has become normalized amongst our boys. And it is just another reason that we have to talk to our guys about the dangers of drug use. They will likely tell you that they know who they're buying from, that these are their friends, that they can trust them. In my experience, most guys believe that this is the case. And they're not necessarily wrong. What they don't fully understand is that someone else sold those drugs to their dealer friends, and someone else sold to them, and on up the chain anyone with access to fentanyl (or some other toxic substance for that matter) can poison our kids.

Again, I share these stories so that you can share them. None of this is fiction. All of this is born of my experience with a lot of teenage boys and young men. The only antidote, which while it's not a sure thing is still our best bet, is communication. When parents openly communicate with their guys about drug use, the likelihood of use and abuse drops precipitously. And with knowledge in hand, our guys are just that much safer. Given the circumstances, I think that's the best story we can write here.

Finally, I urge you to keep in mind that drug use and abuse is not new. Plenty of young men used drugs a generation ago when we were kids. And shaming our kids for using drugs is not at all helpful and is in the end folly. These days, most kids smoke pot or use some other drug. That is just a fact, and I think we all have to open our minds up to that reality in order to communicate effectively with our guys. It's a matter of health and safety, so it needs to be on the table.

The Mass Shooter Problem

"You can't tell me it's not gonna happen at my school, Duffy. You just can't. The way I look at it, it's just a matter of time."

—*Jeremy, fifteen*

Firearms are now the number one cause of death for children and teens in America. Like Jeremy, nearly all of my teenage clients are prepared for a boy their age to walk into school at any time armed with an assault rifle, or two or three of them, bent on killing as many peers as he can, as quickly as he can, and in as violent a manner as he can.

In the wake of mass shootings—and there are plenty of mass shootings—kids head to vigils at their school, in their town, or in the state capital or DC. More and more young people are being politicized and becoming emboldened enough to protest. The kids I work with who attend protests tell me quite calmly that they are fighting for their lives. I think this is an amazing thing about kids today. I remember seeing kids in the week following the shooting at Marjory Stoneman Douglas High School down in Parkland, Florida, taking to microphones within hours and demanding change and gun violence prevention legislation. I was astonished that they had the ability to stand up there and lobby for change. I suspect a lot of us would have been at home working through the trauma of bearing witness to such devastation and destruction. Years later, the strength and courage of these kids continues to amaze me, as they tirelessly take to the podium to speak out in the wake of every new mass shooting, continuing the fight for common sense gun laws week after week and month after month.

Kids are also now in the business of profiling one another, and more than one child has shared with me that they can identify the person or people they think could be shooters at their school: the angry, the bullied, the disenfranchised kid.

And these fellow students they identify are all boys. As I indicated earlier, this is no coincidence. Anyone who inflicts violence on anyone else is responsible for that violence, period. That said, in order to address this problem effectively from a societal point of view, we need to bear down and think upstream, addressing root causes. Too many of our solutions are one-dimensional: "Let's put good guys with guns in the schools." "Let's arm teachers." "Let's take every child with a mental health diagnosis out of school." This last one in particular seems laughable, because while so many bear these diagnoses, only a very small handful of them ever commit violence against someone other than themselves.

I believe we need sweeping change in order to address the proliferation of school shooters. First, I think we need to teach social emotional learning skills in all classrooms from a very young age. Second, I think we need to make our young people, especially our boys, aware that resources within the school are available to them to help them work through their academic or social issues at any time. We need to train teachers, social workers, psychologists, school administrators, and other staff to recognize kids who are struggling or suffering. If we can recognize those signs early on, that sad and lonely boy who feels so terribly hopeless and helpless and urgently needs to be seen will not feel so desperate that he brings a weapon to school to kill. He would receive the help he needs before he becomes that kid. If we can do this, we can save lives. We can save the lives of every victim, as well as the lives of those who become shooters.

I know it's extremely difficult to ask you to extend empathy to those who inflict violence. But remember, they weren't always those kids, and they weren't born that way. This reactive response was triggered in them because they felt like they were nobody. I've worked with more than one boy who has given serious consideration to shooting up his school. Every one of them said they felt like a nonperson, dismissed and unloved. If we can change that for these young men, we can spare many this fear, heartache, death, and devastation, not just for a generation, but maybe forever. Because we can do this.

We must strive with all our might to accomplish this before one more life is extinguished—before one more child is needlessly killed.

The Video Game Problem

"Once I start, I can't seem to stop. I'm so frustrated with myself.
My mom came into my room in the middle of the night,
and I was playing. She said I was breaking her heart."

—*Alex, nineteen*

I don't think there's an issue more frustrating to parents of teenage boys than their use and overuse of video games. Many, many parents have suggested to me that video games are an enormous waste of their son's time. Yet they cannot seem to draw him away from them. Some boys I work with have spent up to six hours a day solely on playing video games. During the pandemic, many boys played even more.

First, let's discuss why boys play video games. If you haven't done so, have a look at the games your son is playing. Video games are incredible now. Have a look at the latest versions of *Final Fantasy*, *Streetfighter*, or *Call of Duty*, and you will be blown away. It may not be your thing, but these games are impressive. The action feels real. Every player has remarkable options they can choose to customize their gaming experience. For around sixty dollars, you have almost countless hours of content to play through, and that's just one version of one single game. Video games are a massive industry for a reason.

Contrary to what many parents believe, video games are also social and interactive. If your son is wearing a headset, he is probably connecting with friends and talking with them within the gaming system. For a lot of boys, this is a primary way that they connect with their friends.

There's also some research supporting the positive aspects of video games for teenagers. They are more active and interactive than simply watching TV, for example. They exert a positive impact on hand-eye coordination over time. Within reason, I find there's nothing wrong with moderate use of video games.

The problem is a lot of boys do not use gaming moderately. And when your son plays video games too much, they can prove pretty damaging. A number of studies show that gaming can be agitating and anxiety inducing when played in excess. They can also drive an increase in feelings of loneliness and even depression. And for better or worse, video games can feel like a haven to boys who have difficulty with focus, attention, and concentration. They tend to find their bearings and are able to concentrate very well on a video game they're interested in.

In the end, I find in my work that excess gaming is in effect a hiding place for boys who are otherwise feeling lost. Most boys are good enough players that they feel a little boost in confidence and self-esteem when they play. They are also freed up from any social concerns outside the game. That is, if they would otherwise feel worried about slipping up and saying the wrong thing when out with people, or the way they look, or the fear of rejection, the game provides a safe haven from all of that. Some boys lack social connections outside gaming altogether, so the video games encapsulate the entirety of their social lives.

I find that this particular group of boys sometimes needs a gentle push in order to find their footing and thrive out in the world. What that looks like is something extracurricular. I don't care whether it is a sport, a stage production, a club, or a job. But if you play the parent card here and get your guy to engage in the world just a little bit, the odds increase enormously that gaming will become less of a necessity to him.

I've said many times that we don't get many parent cards, and we don't. We get fewer as our kids get older. But if your son is playing video games to an excessive degree and is not involved in anything else, it is likely that fear and anxiety are thrumming in the back of his mind. So play the parent card here. Give him the opportunity to connect in a different and far more adaptive and healthy way.

You will likely find that you don't have to eliminate gaming altogether. In fact, I have yet to meet the parents who can. But if he's engaged and connected to people outside of his gaming context, the video games will become what they are supposed to be in the life of your son: a little bit of recreation after a long day of life.

The Sexual Assault Problem

Left to their own devices and thoughts, the boys and young men I work
with hold a deep and abiding respect for the girls and women around
them. They absolutely see them as peers in nearly every way. More and
more boys I work with have very close friends who are girls, unlike
past generations. A lot of boys have noted to me that they can easily
be friends with girls without any pressure for sex or sexual contact.
This is the progress we've been waiting so long for, isn't it? These are
the boys we've been hoping to raise. I've been hearing this wish from
parents for ages.

But the Voices exert a strong impact here. Along with highly
entertaining messages and talk about sports, politics, and culture,
these Voices tend to slip in anger and misogyny. Some of them are
cagey about presenting these messages, while others are absolutely
overt. And our boys are suggestible, especially when they ingest this
content hour after hour every day of their young lives—without a
single counterpoint.

To my thinking, it is here that the Voices are most potent and most
dangerous. We've noted elsewhere in these pages that sexual assaults
on campus and elsewhere are increasing at an alarming rate. Of course,
this is unacceptable behavior. In recent years, we have witnessed a slow
but important course correction. Well-known men who have been
assaulting women for decades are finally getting the comeuppance
they so richly deserve. Many, many women are bravely coming
forward to share their stories, something no one should be compelled
to do. Yet sometimes it seems this is the only way to bring justice to
these criminals. It's so wildly unfair.

And I think we all know that if sexual assault against women is happening in these highly visible areas in major industries, it is happening everywhere. Perhaps naïvely, I'm hoping this course correction eliminates this threat altogether.

Meanwhile, our teenage boys with developing minds are consuming content that either overtly or covertly encourages anger against women. I'm working with far too many boys who feel that anger, and it is not difficult to draw the line that connects that anger to an episode of sexual assault. Unfortunately, I know this to be 100 percent true. I've worked with these situations pretty often in recent years, and in the wake of an assault, the boys I work with cite the Voices as at least a part of their motivation.

As parents, we cannot ignore this phenomenon. It's important that you understand the connection between the Voices your boys internalize and the potential that they might harm another person—or even commit sexual assault against a girl or a young woman. This is another reason it is so imperative that you hear and understand the Voices. Making your own voice heard and providing a counterpoint to their hateful messaging is the only antidote I know. This goes for anyone who has any contact with teenage boys and young men on a regular basis. Ask them what they're consuming in terms of content. Make your voice heard.

This will help your sons right the ship of their thinking. And it will also save your daughters, as well as other girls and young women, from the massive trauma and invasion that is sexual assault. This is so important. Having worked with teenage girls who have experienced sexual assault, it is clear that such assaults can cause a shattering impact on their lives. It can also require decades to get past the trauma and the fear and the anxiety. These events are life altering. Let's do all we can to prevent them.

The Bully Problem

We can conceptualize bullying as boy behavior taken to the extreme. Over the past several years, headlines have focused on online bullying, boys—or girls—calling each other names on social media or attacking each other's reputations or personalities. And yes, this is increasingly common. It's not that our teenagers are cruel per se. It works a lot more like road rage. Because we are not looking somebody straight in the eye and we don't see the pain that we are causing directly, it's easier to tear someone down. When confronted about this directly, most kids express deep regret. And this is not just to save themselves from disapproval in the eyes of their parents or school administrators. The regret is real. I see it here in the therapy room a lot.

But bullying between boys and young men remains a problem. It may not be as rampant as it was a generation ago, but boys can be really directly cruel to one another. I've learned that physical or verbal bullying between boys normally takes place with an audience of other boys. That is, bullies are jockeying for social position and have learned, sometimes through what they've experienced themselves, that this is one way to accomplish that goal. This is nothing to be taken lightly, since bullying can drive boys to anxiety, self-worth issues, suicidal thinking or even suicide.

Not long ago, I worked with David. David is a good-looking guy, a scholar, and an athlete as well. From the outside, it would appear as if he had it all. His family had a nice house in a nice suburb, and he had already been admitted to some top-tier colleges. Not long thereafter, his teammates began to tease him, calling him slow, fat, and stupid. He was, of course, none of these. But the ringleader of the bullying group was persistent. At one point, he asked David if he would be mentioned in David's suicide note.

As we now know, this kind of taunting can be serious, dangerous, and even life-threatening. I am not exaggerating, not in the least, and I think most readers here know that. We also know that this bullying is well beyond trash talking each other or boys just being boys.

We can think of this in a lazy way and simply punish the bullies. But in my experience, that does not stem the tide of bullying. By and large, every bully I have ever known or worked with was bullied himself, either by another child, an older sibling, or his parents, typically a father. The only way he can find to regain his power is to become a bully himself. That is, bullies bully victims, who then become bullies who bully victims. If we recognize this pattern of linkages, we have the opportunity to break it.

So, if you have a child who either is a bully or who has been bullied, you might wonder how we break this cycle. Well, if we have the opportunity to do so, we will start early. And I find that the antidote to bullying is empathy. Kids need to be taught to empathize with other kids who are being bullied, and even to intervene if they witness bullying. But they also need to have the emotional insight and intelligence to recognize when they themselves are the bully. If they—with your help—can come to understand that bullying runs downstream in this way, they can recognize their own role and put an end to it. They can express the pain that they've felt as victims of bullying, either with you, with a capable therapist, or both. This is the way to stem the tide.

Now, I have read books on bullying that suggest brainstorming ways to talk to or evade the bully—tactics that require de facto behavior modification on the part of both parties. In practice, I honestly have not found this to be a very effective method. I actually think we can have a bigger impact on this cultural sickness, and perhaps put an end to it altogether.

Instead, we need to reframe our thinking about bullying altogether. We need to treat both the bully and the bullied as victims. Not that the bully shouldn't be held accountable for his or her actions, for they absolutely should. But in my experience, both kids are in all likelihood victims. Therefore, we must make sure we hear them both out with as open and available a mindset as we can.

The Sports Betting Problem

In putting together a list of parental frustrations with their teenage boys and young men in recent years, sports betting rose to the surface of my mind rather quickly. Boys with no income and no job have no trouble opening accounts with Fan Duel, DraftKings, and most any other sports book. And these sites are so tantalizing. So many of our boys know a lot about sports and are involved in fantasy football and other fantasy teams as early as middle school or younger. Betting on sports feels like a fairly natural extension of their interest in this hobby. And a lot of boys feel like they're not an expert at much, but they do know a lot about sports.

The sports bookies know what they're doing. They offer wild incentives, including what seems to be free money to bet with in order to get kids to sign up for an account. I've noticed that early on, a lot of boys have some surprising luck in their betting. And we all know that early wins simply encourage more and more betting. Other than the fact that it's attached to boys' sports interests, this works no differently than a casino.

To be fair and honest, I'm not 100 percent against sports betting. It does allow boys to demonstrate a certain skill. It can foster some connection between them as they share their bets, wins, and losses. They gather together to watch games and bond through the nature and results of their bets. My clients tell me stories of good-natured ribbing, as when a friend loses a sure thing in the last minutes of the game or match. This is connecting, and to an extent, that is healthy.

Far too many of our boys and young men, however, fall deep down the rabbit hole. Far too often, they over-focus on betting. They check their phones frequently and unconsciously, looking at stats and lines and prepping their bets for the next day, week, or month. In the extreme, they can create some severe financial trouble for themselves. If you find your guys betting too often, be sure to seek out a therapist with some experience in this area. Like so many behaviors, this can become addictive, especially when there's precious little else in a boy or young man's life to feel good about.

But there's another problem with sports betting that raises my concern, and it is far less obvious than addiction. This whole arena creates a universe in which boys and young men fantasize quite often that they may never need to work. A lot of the teenagers I work with think they have a method for beating the system, and in fairness, sometimes they can show me a track record to support that. But the track record is short. That belief is folly.

But it's the infantilization of their thinking that concerns me here. Our boys too often want to hide from the world of actual work. I think we have made it so distasteful to them that they are willing to take any end run around it; so our job in this regard is simple, but not easy. We need to show them, through experience and through our example, that work can be difficult, tiring, frustrating, and everything else that you might experience in your own workday.

But just as importantly, if not more so, we need to show them that work can be joyful. We need to demonstrate that work can be rewarding, that work can be not just a job, but a vocation. If we don't do that, our boys will just look for other ways to navigate an escape from work. And through gambling and other methods, a lot of them are actively doing so.

Let's not forget that our boys have an awful lot to offer the world. Yet far too many of them don't want anything to do with discovering and sharing their gifts. Part of this is on us, especially us dads.

So pick out a "bring your son to work" day, even if your company doesn't have one. Show the boy in your life what you do at work, and if you have the opportunity, have him participate. Provide him with jobs to do around the house. Encourage him to get a part-time job outside of the house. No matter what, allow him the opportunity to discover the rewards that work can bring into his life. By doing so, you will be mitigating the difficulties that are not only fed by sports betting, but by so many other distractions. This is an important role that we parents have to serve in the lives of our boys.

Part Five

The Solutions

Your Boy's Relationship with You

"I love my parents, man. I really do.
But I can't talk to them. They don't get me at all."

—*Travis, seventeen*

I've worked with so many parents who want the best for their guys, but who feel powerless to change their negative feelings about themselves or their negative, self-defeating behaviors. I don't know if there's a more difficult place for a parent to come from than a feeling of powerlessness when they can tell their guy is suffering.

If you're in that situation, I do have good news for you. Research shows—and my experience supports—that you as a parent remain the single most powerful influence on the thoughts and behaviors of your sons. If you're skeptical, I totally get it. How exactly are you supposed to exert this supposed influence? You may feel like everything you say to him goes in one ear and out the other. I get it.

This is where the concept of the emotional bank account comes in, and its importance cannot be overstated. So hang in here with me for a moment. Every single relationship we engage in generates an emotional bank account. So, if we have more negative than positive interactions with each other, that emotional bank account will have a negative balance. We will be in the red—and everything about that relationship will seem trying and difficult.

If, however, we've generated some goodwill in any relationship, be it with a spouse, friend, work associate, or our child, that account carries a balance in the black. And as a result, things are going to go far more smoothly in that relationship. You and your spouse will find common ground more readily. You and your work associate will iron out differences with ease. And your child will listen when you need him to hear you, when his health and safety are at risk, or his behavior is heading into dangerous territory, or he seems to be struggling emotionally. The emotional bank account is the most powerful tool you have available to you as a parent.

So, you might be wondering, especially if you are in the red with your son, how do you create a positive balance in the account for this relationship? All you need to do to increase that balance, even if it's deep in the red and you feel like there's no way to turn it around, is to connect with him.

Get to know his world. Sit down and listen to what he's listening to, watch what he's watching, play what he's playing. Let him teach you how TikTok works or how you level up in his video game. Let him tell you what it's like to be a teenager today, the social difficulties, the academic stressors, and all of it. Spend a *lot* of time with him. Most of your time spent parenting is not parenting at all. It's just connecting with your guy. Keep in mind that this connection is crucial to him right now in his teenage years. He needs that relationship with you to lean on so he is allowed to feel like a kid again when the world he lives in just feels like too much.

If you can get there, he will feel he has an ally and a guide and a consultant in these most difficult, anxiety-inducing times, and he will feel some agency in his life. And the more you get to know him, the better you'll feel about who he is. Chances are, if my experience serves, that you'll find your guy is far deeper, more thoughtful, likable, lovable, talented, and smart than you have any idea he is. Let him show these sides of his character to you.

But if you need additional incentive, I want you to keep in mind that you are not just laying the foundation for helping guide him through his teenage years. You're creating a connection that will last a lifetime. When I wrote my first book, my son was fourteen and I was in the thick of the teenage years with him. Now, he's twenty-seven years old. And because my wife Julie and I attended to that emotional bank account with George, we are close to him now. Julie and I are the best of friends with him and his fiancé Lauren. We hang out with them as often as we do anyone else in our lives. Our connection with them brings us more joy than we can tell you.

And I think we can both attest that you won't regret a moment of making deposits in the emotional bank account.

The Value of Work

One interesting trend I've noticed in my practice over the last several years is that fewer and fewer teenage boys seem to hold jobs. This trend toward inertia actually concerns me quite a bit, in large part because it drives a couple of other disturbing trends. First, more and more boys are missing out on the enormous value that work can provide for them. Sure, young men who work get paid, so they get a feel for the value of money; but just as importantly, if not more so, they get a feel for their own sense of competence and resilience.

Those initial jobs tend to open the eyes of teenagers to what is possible for them. Through the feedback they receive, they realize they are capable and competent. They also hear about areas in which they can improve and can work toward doing a better job. And they may learn that they don't like menial work all that much, so they may engage more in school. These are critical life skills that too many of our boys are missing.

I'm especially concerned about boys who don't do particularly well in school. Too many of them reach high school graduation without ever hearing direct feedback on how they're doing. Therefore, these young men often have no bead on their sense of their own competence or their resilience in difficult circumstances. A job can sometimes provide a sense of self and of self-worth that school cannot.

For those who are concerned about your boys playing too many video games, smoking or vaping too much, or staring at their phones too often, time spent on the job drives all of this stuff into the margins of their lives. This is a big deal, because a job may eliminate the perceived need for one or more of those activities in their day. In my opinion and my experience, a job adds some color and dynamism to boys' sometimes bland and boring lives.

Expert Tip: Get a Job

If your son has time on his hands and spends way too much time in a state of inertia, encourage him to pursue a job. When I was in high school, my best friend Mike had a job in the produce department of a local grocery store. An opening came up, and he encouraged me to interview for it. I did so, and my life became so much richer for that experience.

I remember marveling at my first paycheck and feeling so proud of that accomplishment and the feeling of earning something. It really meant something to me. I had to learn to engage with the public in a pretty professional way. This is an important lesson. I had to learn a whole new structure of spending time: when to be on task and when to take it a little bit easier. The work was dynamic, and in the end, really enjoyable. I made good friendships and have workplace stories that I still tell.

So let's give our sons the opportunity for that same experience. We know it proves to be of value in many ways.

Case Study: Camp Doug

"I don't know how to do anything!
Isn't that part of being a man?"

—Alex, seventeen

As parents, we want our boys to feel capable and competent. Too often, though, many of our guys are presented with precious few opportunities to show that to themselves and to others. A lot of boys have expressed what Alex told me that day. They don't feel like they know how to do anything in the real world. Some of the abilities we attach to masculinity through stereotype are in fact crucial for our boys in order to feel smart, capable, responsible, and resilient.

But most teenage boys will tell me they know how to navigate social media. They can work most computer applications pretty well, and they are really adept at video games. But as one boy put it to me recently, "I don't know how to hammer a nail or use a drill. I can't change a tire or fix an engine. I really don't know how to do anything men are supposed to know how to do."

This is a familiar sentiment among boys. I hear this from some girls as well, but far more from boys.

I have friends with a lake house up in Wisconsin, and my family and I are invited up frequently. Doug, a native Wisconsinite, has lived with his family in the same area his entire life. He buys land and works on it. He has every type of heavy machinery one can imagine. During the pandemic, he decided to build a tiny house in one of his many pole barns. So he did. By himself. He built one.

A whole house.

I've asked Doug many times whether he would consider leading a Man Camp for some of the boys I work with. I think they could learn a lot from him about how to do things, about the discipline required to get them done. They could learn about setting goals and keeping schedules and building things with their hands.

I truly think these faculties are missing from the lives of far too many of our boys. When I work with a young man who builds something on his own, who exercises that disciplined power, they learn something about what they're made of. They can look at what they've made and feel proud of it.

I don't think this is a fringe issue. It is clear that many, many boys are unsure about the nature of masculinity, but most would agree that the ability to work hard in a physical way is a part of it. I don't think we have a disagreement on that. I work with one young man, Colton, whose dad is very handy with tools, building, and projects around the house and the yard. Colton typically resists helping at every turn. After he got into some trouble with his parents over the course of the last school year, he spent the summer trying to make up for it by offering to help out around the house. During this time with his dad, he learned how to build and create and get up early and work and sweat. And to his enormous surprise, he actually really enjoyed it.

He felt he accomplished a lot. He felt capable and competent. But he also felt the impact of difficult labor and problem-solving. Not incidentally, Colton noted that he spent more time outside, breathing fresh air and sweating with effort, than he can ever remember.

As previously discussed here, so many of our boys are medicated just for being boys, for being physical and for having difficulty paying attention while sitting still in a classroom. But this type of camp, whether it's an organized event or a makeshift affair at home, can be so useful in elevating boys' self-esteem and cementing an experiential basis for their definition of masculinity. It may also decrease or eliminate the perceived need for him to be prescribed medication to cope. We need to find ways to provide our boys with this type of opportunity. If we do, you will see the fog of depression, anxiety, and attention problems lift with his energy. I can't remember the last time a boy did not rise to this occasion.

The Value of Movement

Along with work, I've also witnessed a precipitous decline in extracurricular activity in the teenage boys I work with. This is a real bummer, as those extracurriculars can provide a number of positives that school alone cannot. I find that teenage boys are more balanced—emotionally, physically, spiritually, and otherwise—when they are involved in active pursuits and feel they are a part of something bigger than themselves. After-school clubs, sports, student government, plays, marching bands, or any other activities make for a far better story than scrolling through social media alone behind a closed door.

Boys in particular need movement. I find that boys who are involved in a team sport fare far better emotionally than boys who are not. Many boys gain confidence by mastering a skill on a court or playing field, in a pool, or at the gym. They can gauge their improvement and how it matches the degree of effort they put in. This mastery over their own body's ability to do something remarkable is really important for our boys. For those not involved in sports, this piece is frequently missing. It's an important piece.

We also need to recognize how important it is for our boys to move. My clients who are home too much are anxious and lethargic at the same time. They rarely report that they feel good either physically or emotionally. Movement is so important for our boys' bodies during these years. You simply cannot overestimate its importance.

Physical Touch and Intimacy

"I can't remember the last time I felt the touch
of another person. Not a girl, not my mom,
definitely not my dad. Nobody."

—Emmett, eighteen

I don't often think to ask teenage boys about physical touch, but when Emmett said the above, it really struck me. I asked several other teenage boys over the next couple of weeks when they were last touched or had last touched another human being. All of them said they couldn't remember. All of them.

A while back, I was on a radio show with another psychologist who is an expert on physical touch. She described the many benefits of a hug, a hand on the shoulder, a held hand, a kiss, and other kinds of physical touch and how important this is to our well-being. She pointed out that newborns in neonatal ICU units often require skin-to-skin touch in order to survive—not just thrive, but survive. And she said we never really lose that need.

After the radio segment, we stuck around and talked for a while. I told her about my teenagers. She asked if the girls experience the same dearth of touch as the boys, and I laughed. Of course not. Girls hug each other all the time. They will hold hands walking down the hall.

They touch their siblings and parents. And I told her what Emmett, the boy quoted above, had told me: Save for an occasional high-five, they never touch anyone else, and they are never touched.

She further asked about girlfriends, and I realized that, in the past several years, the vast majority of boys I worked with not only weren't in relationships, but they didn't show interest in them. Only a few years back, I can remember spending large swathes of sessions talking to boys who were excited about the prospect of being in a relationship. They had that awesome, exciting, life filled adolescent juice that wanted nothing more than to connect with another person, through touch and otherwise. Now, I think a lot of boys actively avoid that situation. Some of this has to do with the porn our boys consume.

Many boys just fear intimacy of any kind. They don't know how to be intimate and vulnerable and open and fully themselves with another person. Their sense of this is dulled by the pornography they watch; that important, crucial, joyful, adolescent energy is pent up within them. Therefore, instead of that energy manifesting in them through intimacy and touch, boys hold it in, resulting in anxiety and agitation, and sometimes depression.

It is critical that boys get familiar with this gentler side of themselves, the side that wants to touch others and wants to be touched, physically and otherwise. As parents, we do have an opportunity to open some of those doors. We can engage in emotionally open discussions with our sons. We can hug them.

Like many men of his generation, my own father was not affectionate and did not share his feelings very readily at all. But every night that I can remember, he kissed each of us on the forehead. For my siblings, and I, this was a crucial introduction into intimacy and connection.

That simple kiss allowed us permission to want that physical touch and that intimate connection.

Consider for a moment what you want for your son in this regard. Intimacy, physical touch, and even a deep sexual connection at the right time in his life are probably not the most comfortable areas for us to talk about with our sons. But they are so important. I encourage you to wade into that discomfort. Hug your sons. At the very least, kiss them on the forehead at the end of the day and tell them that you love them. Doing this will provide them with a hint of what they want, and what they want to provide in their relationships going forward in their lives. We all want that for them, don't we?

Relationships

"Girls hold all the cards in relationships. Screw that.
I'd rather not."

—James, sixteen

Just a few short years ago, the boys I worked with were spending a significant part of their therapy sessions talking about relationships. Most of my young male clients felt that flutter of excitement, attraction, and maybe a little anxiety around a certain girl, or sometimes a certain boy.

We would talk about whether he might text her, approach her at a party or a football game, or ask her out. I suspect anyone reading remembers similar passages in their own teenage years. And these are important times for our kids and their later relationships. Beginning to get a feel for the type of person you're drawn to and the type of person you're not is an important ritual as well as a crucial stage of development. It also begins to calibrate an internal guide for how to be in a relationship, now and in the future. It's no small thing.

Once they were in a relationship, it was fascinating to see how teenagers would manage it. How often would they text each other? Do they FaceTime every night with each other? When do they kiss? Do they feel they want to go further sexually, and how is that determined? Are they exclusive with one another, or can they date other people? At what point will they call each other boyfriend or girlfriend? How do they determine when a relationship has run its course and it's time to break up? All of these experiences are really important rites of passage.

The majority of the teenage boys I work with today, however, really don't talk about intimate relationships at all. Some of them go through high school—and even the rest of their teen years—never being in a relationship, never overtly wanting to be in one. Now, some of you parents may look at this as a bit of relief. Without relationships, you don't have to worry about whether your son is going to have sex. You don't have to be concerned about unwanted pregnancy or the heartbreak of a relationship ending.

You may even feel like it spares you the sex talk! (It does not.)

In the end, we don't want our boys to be skipping these steps. Some recent studies have shown that fewer men under thirty-five are in relationships, and young men are having less sex than ever before. This is not good news. Relationships and sex are healthy. In my experience, teenagers can lean on their relationships. They steady themselves emotionally when they're in a relationship. In my experience, this is even more true for teen boys than girls.

In fact, my experience and that of my colleagues would suggest that boys are more on task, more motivated, more engaged, and less depressed and anxious when in a relationship. They take better care of themselves, physically and emotionally. They're more likely to exercise and eat well. They are less likely to use recreational drugs and far less likely to use them in excess.

So, what can we do as parents? Well, the Voices have a way of turning boys off to relationships, especially with girls. Too many of our teenage boys have a negative feeling about girls in general. I've heard the following sentiments from teenage boys in the past couple of years:

- "They hold all the cards in a relationship, sexually and otherwise."

- "They are trying to rob us of our power."

- "They have the ability to emasculate us."

- "They can accuse us of sexual assault any time and ruin our reputations."

Shockingly, none of these beliefs are unusual. We as parents therefore need to talk to our sons about their feelings toward girls and women. We need to provide a counterpoint to the Voices' potent influences since they can poison our boys' minds against girls. We need to share our feelings about the positive attributes of both genders. If we don't get our voices in the mix, these other Voices may very well set the tone for their attitudes.

If your son is in a healthy relationship, I encourage you to be supportive. Invite their partners over for dinner. Get to know them. Let's make this a playful, enjoyable experience for our guys. We have the ability to turn the tide here, and we don't want the window on that opportunity to close before we effect some change.

Finally, it appears as if the Voices exert a powerful influence on
relationships between boys and girls and between young men and
young women. Many of the girls I work with told me they would love
to be in a relationship with a boy, but that many of the boys they know
are absorbing hateful, misogynistic, nihilistic content into their brains.
A recent study suggests that more than half of heterosexual Millennial
and Gen Z women consider listening to the Joe Rogan podcast a red
flag in a potential partner. And I'll remind you, a shocking number of
young men and boys listen to this podcast.

Curiously, a number of other red flags were cited: claiming to be
MAGA, demonstrating homophobia or suggesting there are only
two genders, and even a refusal to see the *Barbie* movie. For our
girls and young women, all of these suggest not only a closed mind,
but, from what girls are telling me, a dangerous mind. These girls
do not feel safe with boys who hold these beliefs. They don't think
a healthy relationship will ensue with such a boy, and they feel they
have precious little in common with them. So, the fact that recently
boys are in relationships with girls far less often is due at least in part
to the Voices. This is another crucial reason that we need to provide a
counter-voice to such content, because our boys are listening to it far
more than we know.

Friendships and Social Lives

If you get a chance, take a look at how groups of teenage girls hang out
with one another. There are few sights more dynamic than a group of
teenage girls. They trade compliments, raise each other up, and openly
celebrate each other. Girls are physical with one another. They hug
and hold and lean on each other—a lot. Now, I know that groups of
girls are not as simple and homogenous as that. I know they're very
dynamic and different from one another. I know girls can be really,

really cruel to each other as well. But among girls, I've seen bullies and victims manage to work things out with each other and rekindle a friendship. Others just decide to remain apart, each in their own group, but separate.

In the therapy room, teenage girls describe deep, connected relationships. They can share most anything with their friends, and they frequently do. At times, I worry that some girls take on too much responsibility for their friends' emotional lives. They are de facto therapists for one another, and at times I worry that some emotional problem will become too heavy for them to carry. But they are eager to serve as ports in the storm for each other.

Some teenage boy friendships look a lot like this as well. A few boys I work with tell me of deep and meaningful connections with their friends. As I've indicated elsewhere here, the deepening of those male friendships often comes in the wake of something difficult or tragic happening in the lives of one or more of the boys. But on the whole, relative to teenage girls, friendships between teenage boys tend to be somewhat superficial in nature. Boys don't often engage in deep conversations with one another. Many of them tell me that, even over the course of a night in a buddy's basement, playing video games or watching movies, guys tend to say very little to one another. Boys can be energetically physical with each other, as they are conditioned to give each other a hard time. They might wrestle, slap, or, on occasion, high-five each other, but that's often the extent of their physical contact with friends.

Boys also create in-jokes together via memes and GIFs shared on Snapchat and other, newer platforms like Discord and TikTok. They talk to each other in multiplayer video games, within that online context. But deep, meaningful conversations about the nature of their relationships and how they feel, the complexities of family, and navigating an approach to adult life, these are things that boys hold deep inside. Of course, this lack of connection can result in dangerous and unhealthy isolation that devolves rather readily into depression, hopelessness, and anxiety for some of them.

Suffice it to say, the vast majority of our boys are not deep in the practice of sharing with each other. That's part of the reason that so many boys, even those who have some good friends, feel lonely and disconnected. We haven't taught them to connect well, and our boys are left with precious few close friendships, if any.

That's not to say that boys don't need to feel that same sense of belonging that girls enjoy. They absolutely do. Rich, meaningful social lives are essential to them, just as much as they are for girls. The good news is this can start at home. If we start talking more deeply with our boys, and if we model for them what it's like to talk about their feelings, they are likely to take that process into their friendships. If you need any incentive to change the nature of your relationships at home, here it is. Set the tone with deeper discussions at home, and those truly do tend to radiate out into other relationships.

Because the last thing we want for our boys is a set of disconnected relationships that don't serve them emotionally. These relationships can only leave them feeling more lonely and socially isolated, with no place to put any distress they might be suffering other than inside. Let's help them create and participate in relationships that are meaningful— ones they can lean on, both at home and with their friends. This again is the better story.

If we're to engage in a full discussion about the socialization of boys, it would be a mistake to ignore social media, video games, and the Discord platform, which provides opportunities for online social interaction simultaneously with gaming. In moderation, these are both very common and reasonable ways for boys to connect with one another. Some of my teenage clients have told me they share some of their deepest conversations with their friends via one or both of these online contexts. They have proven to be far better communication tools than we might think. Both social media and video games allow our boys to share in a less intimate context than in a face-to-face conversation, where they may be far less likely to share confidences. That's the good news.

The downside is that these venues for online communication encourage more of the same superficial, jokey connections that boys typically share face-to-face. This may afford them a quick chuckle, but it doesn't do a whole lot to make them feel any more connected.

There are also some risks associated with both of these types of communication platforms. An errant post on any online conversation may seem benign in context, but come across in a very different way taken out of context, and the potential consequences can be troubling. If someone takes a screenshot of an offending comment or records only part of a video game discussion, it can be shared and even go viral more rapidly than you would believe possible. We need to talk with our boys about the potential for these problems, as I've worked with a number of them who have created significant social trouble for themselves through what they may have thought was a confidential communication between friends. Some can even get into significant trouble with their school, including suspension or even expulsion as possible disciplinary actions. I worked with a few boys who had gotten into legal trouble online by sharing a lewd thought about a female classmate or talking too openly about drug abuse.

Sidebar: Encouraging Cooperation and Communication Between the Genders

Right now, we are in the midst of a massive gender divide among young people that is not only toxic but growing exponentially rapidly. In my practice, I am bearing witness to an increase in resentment month by month and year over year, especially in the way boys and young men feel about girls and young women. I am finding, more and more, boys hang out with only other boys, both during the week and on the weekends. Or boys may hang out alone in their rooms or basements, whiling the time away, but too often developing toxic mindsets with nobody present to bounce their new ideas off of. And without the option of being with the boys, girls hang out only with girls, or nearly so.

This dynamic allows for precious little time for the genders to connect, other than at parties and through hookups that tend not to move the needle of understanding in a positive direction.

The Usefulness of Therapy

In the introduction, I talked about the difference in the ways in which boys and girls approach therapy. And it's all true. Girls tend to embrace the therapy hour gladly, without any shame whatsoever. They tend to bring in an agenda with them and complete any assigned homework. Girls are really good at therapy even when they're having a very difficult time.

It's also true that boys, on the whole, tend to struggle in the therapy hour. They often approach the hour skittishly, like they might be in trouble. They resist talking about their emotions, or they struggle to do so. They tolerate the hour, but they don't lean into it nor engage with the process of therapy as efficiently as girls do.

We've talked about some of the reasons for this. First, boys are in general not as well equipped with emotional language as girls are, so they don't necessarily know what to say. Needing therapy might also feel like a sign of weakness to some boys. Some of them have told me that directly. In the same vein, a lot of boys feel that therapy is in essence more feminine than masculine, contributing to their reluctance to engage.

And honestly, they might be right about that. Therapy engages a softer and gentler side of us. As I've suggested before, we may need to integrate some of these feminine qualities into our definition of masculinity in order to create space for our boys to really happily thrive.

No, I don't think therapy is the answer to everything. We shouldn't be in therapy perpetually. But I would propose that a lot of our boys would benefit from therapy. In the past couple of years, I have received calls from a few parents, all moms, asking if I would see their sons for therapy. Some of these boys were as young as nine or ten years old. When I asked one mom what the presenting problem was, that is, what her son was struggling with, she told me he really wasn't struggling with much of anything. She wanted him to connect with a therapist to remove the taboo around the process so that if and when he ever wanted to get into therapy, he would look at it as a tool that he could tap into without shame anytime.

I decided to make space for some of these boys, and the results have been pretty remarkable. I'm finding that when we get to boys early enough, we can not only remove the taboo around therapy, we can also get them to look forward to it as well. They begin to learn the emotional language that's been missing and start to develop those emotional intelligence skills they may have been lacking. I've been surprised to find that therapy served as a pretty solid jumpstart for these boys, allowing them to start to catch up with their female peers organically.

I'm therefore going to encourage you to get your sons involved in therapy. Make sure the therapist has experience in working with teenage boys and their resistance to emotional engagement. Talk to the therapist beforehand about what your son is like and what the therapist can expect. The more prepared they are, the more effective therapy can be. There is no better way that I know to bridge that emotional intelligence gap than for teenage boys to talk about themselves and the way they feel in an environment that was designed just for that. It may be taxing at first, and your guy might resist or resent it, but he won't regret it. Over time, boys warm up to the idea and engage.

It's really important for boys to develop the ability to recognize when they might need help and to reach out and get it—in my view, this is a crucial skill. Young men whom I worked with when they were teenagers sometimes call to come in for a few sessions if they're struggling with something in their life. Because they were in therapy when they were younger, finding help for themselves in the emotional sphere is not foreign; it is familiar. For these men, therapy doesn't feel like weakness, it feels like a tool, and it bolsters and strengthens them. And that is so healthy. We definitely want this for our boys and young men. So, set up a session for your boys.

Calling on All Dads and Men

"I love my dad, man, but I don't want a life like his. I think he's miserable. I think he hates his job. And he never, ever seems to have any fun at all. I'm afraid of that kind of life."

—Jack, seventeen

Gentlemen, I wanted to address you directly since you make the single greatest impression on the feelings and attitudes of your sons and the young men in your lives. I need to share a difficult truth or two with you. First, you need to know that many, many of the teenage boys I work with do not want the lives their fathers have presented to them. They are paying close attention to you, whether you know it or not. They see and hear you when you say that you hate your job, that you're financially burdened by your family, or that you're just plain unhappy in your life. They pay attention to the way you treat women—their mothers in particular—and that shapes the foundation for how they will treat women more than any other factor, period. If at the end of a long day, the first thing you do is grab a drink, you cannot be too surprised when your son reaches for alcohol or his drug of choice.

So, it is incumbent upon you to provide a hopeful space for his future.

I feel for the men of my generation. I suspect that like mine, your fathers were or are good men. But they may not have connected with you, at least not when you were a teenager. They may well have been distant, remote, and stern faced—far from emotionally available. In all likelihood, you were never provided with an example of how to embody this touchy-feely stuff I'm asking you to embrace.

Note that your boys are growing up in a different and far harsher world. And they are exposed to every dark corner of it, at far younger ages than any of us could possibly have been. So, I want you to keep in mind that your boys need you to provide a pathway toward a hopeful future for them. They don't have that now. They cannot see that from where they are. And most of us are not showing them by example that it is even a possibility for them.

So what I am going to ask of you is to reconnect with your joy and bliss, or discover them for the first time. Find your happiness and your peace. If you've given up on your physical self, lace up the running shoes and get back out there. If you put an instrument down decades ago, pick it back up, tune it up, and give it another try. Show your guys that work also can be a source of goodness and joy and contribution to the greater good. If you find you are filled with self-pity, demonstrate for them how to find the best even in difficult situations. If you find you need to see a therapist to get you there, seek one out. Let your boy know you're doing so, and why. That will serve as a positive example for him, solid modeling of problem-solving emotional difficulties, and removal of a persistent taboo.

Thoreau once said, "The mass of men lead lives of quiet desperation." What was quite likely true in his day has become a more profound reality in the generations since. With a little self-awareness, we have the rare opportunity right now to turn the tide—not just for ourselves, but for our boys and young men and the generations following them.

This will be so good for your boys, but it will be good for you too. We all know that men tend to lead shorter lives than women, and arguably not only far shorter but far less happy lives at that. Let's see if we can catch up a little bit in our generation.

A few years back, I was talking with a group of men at a neighborhood party. They complained about being stuck in the linear "breadwinner and provider" story. They would stand around the fire pit with not much to say, drinking beer and laughing about the beer they'd consumed the night before. The entire evening left me feeling sad, hollow, and lifeless.

I recognized that night that far too many men don't feel alive. Whereas in middle age, many women tend to reinvent and reinvigorate their lives, many of us men fail to do so.

But if we revitalize our own lives, we take some of the weight of terror off the shoulders of our sons. We offer them some excitement about their futures. We have to part the gray clouds that adulting looks like to them. We can give our boys a gift. We have to.

And finally, it's highly important for us as fathers to foster the softer side of our boys. That's where some of their strength lies. Think of men you admire and the moments in which you have most admired them. It's likely not in those big, loud moments with their chest puffed out pridefully. It was almost certainly in the quieter, more vulnerable moments, when they are most open and available. That's when we respect men the most. Show that side of yourself to your boys. That will provide them permission to show that side of themselves to others.

Part Six

Conclusion

As you can probably tell, I'm a big fan of our teenage boys. To a man, they are remarkable human beings: kind, thoughtful, funny, intelligent, and strong. I want more of them to see these qualities in themselves, because far, far too often they miss that. So, if nothing else, I urge you to echo these sentiments with your guy. Let him know all the good that you see in him even if he doesn't see it himself. Encourage all the shifts and behavior change that we've talked about here, but treat him gently. He's got a lot on his mind. He needs to know that you are there and available for him, no matter what. His well-being depends on that.

I very much appreciate you taking the time and care to read this book. I am extremely concerned about the suffering of our young men, and I hope we have shone a light here both on the nature of that suffering and what we can do to alleviate the majority of it. I need you to know that wherever you are with your son, your situation is not hopeless. So if he is not going to school, if he's smoking or drinking too much, or if he is belligerent toward you and disengaged at home, do not give up on him. Hang in there with him. Begin to repair and rebuild and communicate and connect. Let him know you're not going anywhere, and neither is he. Let him know that you love him unconditionally, no matter who he is and no matter what he does.

And please don't make too many assumptions about his thoughts or behavior. Go for understanding. Meet your boy where he is without blame or shame. Just your open heart and open mind will do. And if he tells you what's on his mind or what he's struggling with, believe him. Even if it's really hard to hear, believe him. Grounded in truth, you can carry on together.

I want you to envision, just for a moment, softening your approach with him. The world is harsh for our kids. They're exposed to way too much, way too early in their lives. They are sensitive to the needs of others, across the table at the next desk, or even across the globe. So our kids, and most especially our boys, need our gentleness. Let them soften. Let them regress a little bit at home. Be a sanctuary they seek out, not an impediment they avoid.

We clearly need advocacy for our boys, a revolution of sorts. As parents and caregivers, you can help start this process on a micro scale—in a boy to boy, parent to parent, house to house transformation. You can be parenting trailblazers here, with just a few simple but critical shifts. Listen more than you speak. Use emotional language when you talk with your boys. Encourage them to keep an open mind by doing so yourself. Hug them frequently. Show them your unconditional positive regard for them on the most trying day. Bring gentleness, quiet, and stability into their loud, harsh, unpredictable world. These few interventions will make all the difference, and just might ignite a revolution of change our boys desperately need.

Resource Guide:

Essential Tools for Supporting Disaffected Teen Boys

This Resource Guide was created to complement *Rescuing Our Sons: 8 Solutions to Our Crisis of Disaffected Teen Boys*. If you're a parent, an educator, a mental health professional, a guardian, or another individual who recognizes the importance of nurturing young men in our contemporary society, this guide is tailored specifically for you. The teenage years—a transformative phase of growth and self-discovery—have always been complex. But with the dawn of the digital age, evolving societal norms, and unique modern-day challenges, the intricacies have only intensified, especially for our boys. This prompted us to craft a guide that offers clarity, support, and, most critically, actionable resources to empower you to help these young minds.

At its core, this Resource Guide serves two primary purposes: First, it acts as an extended hand to the concepts elucidated in *Rescuing Our Sons*. While the book lays an invaluable foundation by dissecting the primary challenges and suggesting viable solutions, this guide aims to translate those insights into tangible actions. It achieves this by directing you toward extensive studies, in-depth discussions, expert commentaries, and organizations that are tirelessly working to address the many concerns of our disaffected teen boys. Second, this guide is a heartfelt attempt to cultivate community. It strives to bridge connections—linking you to a vast network of professionals, ushering you toward platforms that facilitate insightful peer exchanges, and highlighting channels that offer fresh, research-backed insights, tools, and strategies that revolve around the holistic well-being of teen boys.

As you read this guide, engage, interact, and immerse yourself. We've included a list of enlightening podcasts that merge learning with leisure and have highlighted dedicated organizations that provide specialized programs tailored for young men. Perhaps you'll find value in joining specific support networks or online communities where mutual experiences are shared, questions are posed, solutions are brainstormed, and collective growth is celebrated. Given the ever-evolving landscape of the digital world and our ever-adaptive society, many resources, especially online platforms and forums, undergo frequent updates. To stay up to date, consider strategies like periodic check-ins, setting reminders, bookmarks, or even opting for newsletter subscriptions.

Supporting our disaffected teen boys isn't just about addressing challenges; it's about envisioning a brighter, more hopeful future. It's about recognizing potential, fostering resilience, and igniting passion. With this guide, we empower you with knowledge, resources, and a community spirit. Every piece of information, every tool, and every connection is a step toward building a world where our young men thrive—a future brimming with promise.

Podcasts

Navigating the intricate landscape of the teenage years can be daunting for parents, guardians, educators, and mentors, particularly when boys grapple with unique societal expectations and personal challenges. Podcasts have emerged as a cornerstone for guidance, offering expert perspectives, relatable stories, and practical advice. Easily accessible during a commute, a workout, or even daily chores, these audio resources provide timely insights, empathy, and, often, solutions to the dilemmas faced by parents and guardians. Below is a carefully curated list of podcasts illuminating the nuances of parenting, understanding, and championing teen boys in their journey to adulthood.

The Art of Manliness

Hosted by Brett McKay, this podcast dives into various topics central to men's lifestyle and self-improvement. It touches on masculinity, mental well-being, and life challenges, providing listeners with well-researched and thought-provoking content. www.artofmanliness.com/podcast

Building Boys

Jennifer L. W. Fink and Janet Allison come together to shed light on the intricacies of raising boys. They delve into education, behavior, and the societal pressures boys face today, offering actionable insights and solutions for parents and caregivers. buildingboys.net

Dad Edge Podcast

This podcast ventures into the realms of fatherhood, spotlighting the importance of positive masculinity. It encourages mental well-being and emphasizes cultivating a deeper, more meaningful bond with children. thedadedge.com/podcast

The Longest Shortest Time

Created by Hillary Frank, this award-winning podcast unravels the complexities of parenthood. It features episodes that specifically address understanding teenagers, offering insights and strategies to navigate the often-challenging teen years. longestshortesttime.com

Mindful Parenting in a Messy World

This podcast offers a refreshing take on how mindfulness techniques can support parents during the tumultuous teenage years. It presents strategies to stay centered, calm, and responsive to the unique needs of teens. authenticparenting.com/mindful-parenting-messy-world

Mighty Mommy

Mighty Mommy serves as a treasure trove of practical advice for parents. It transforms parenting from an overwhelming task to an enjoyable journey, offering tips and tricks grounded in real-life experiences. www.mightymommas.net/national-podcasts

Mighty Parenting

Targeting the challenges of raising teens and young adults in today's fast-paced world, this podcast provides actionable solutions. It addresses common issues and offers insights to empower parents and guardians. mightyparenting.com/podcast

Mom and Dad Are Fighting

Offering a candid look into parenting, this podcast discusses the highs and lows of raising teenagers. It combines personal anecdotes with expert opinions, giving listeners a holistic view of teen parenthood. podcasts.apple.com/us/podcast/mom-and-dad-are-fighting-slates-parenting-show/id774383607

Mom Enough: Parenting Tips, Research-Based Advice, and a Few Personal Confessions

This podcast balances expert interviews and heartfelt personal stories. It offers listeners research-based advice, lively discussions, and relatable confessions from moms who've successfully navigated parenting. podcasts.google.com/feed/aHR0cHM6Ly9tb21lbm91Z2guY29tL2ZlZWQvcG9kY2FzdA

The Modern Dads Podcast

This podcast delves into various parenting topics, with particular emphasis on promoting positive masculinity and comprehending the teenage brain. It's a valuable resource for fathers and other caregivers seeking more profound insights into their roles. open.spotify.com/show/3I3XeOODZweOpcxCchyPFl

Parenting Great Kids with Dr. Meg Meeker

Dr. Meg Meeker takes listeners through a variety of parenting topics. She provides expert advice and practical strategies, primarily focusing on raising confident, resilient children, including teenage boys. podcasts.apple.com/us/podcast/parenting-great-kids-with-dr-meg-meeker/id1101900764

Parenting Teens: The Biggest Job We'll Ever Have

Offering profound insights into teen parenting, this podcast sheds light on the challenges and the rewards. It's a resourceful platform for parents, drawing from over four decades of expert experience with teens. www.iheart.com/podcast/263-parenting-teens-the-28753062

Parenting Today's Teens Podcast

This daily podcast, hosted by Mark Gregston, is a gem for anyone involved in teen parenting. With over forty-five years of experience, Gregston shares invaluable advice, strategies, and insights to foster better relationships with teens. podcasts.apple.com/us/podcast/parenting-todays-teens/id1518750946

Power Your Parenting: Moms With Teens

Dedicated solely to guiding moms through the adolescent years, this podcast provides strategies, advice, and reassurance. It's a supportive space for mothers facing the challenges of raising teenagers. podcasts. apple.com/us/podcast/power-your-parenting-moms-with-teens/ id842121985

Respectful Parenting: Janet Lansbury Unruffled

Janet Lansbury's podcast, while primarily centered on younger children, offers invaluable advice for parenting teenagers. It advocates for a respectful, understanding approach to parenting, ensuring both the parent and the teen feel heard and validated. www.janetlansbury. com/podcast-audio

Understood: For Learning and Thinking Differences

This podcast for parents of children who learn and think differently explores the unique challenges such children and teenagers face, offering insights, strategies, and support. www.understood. org/podcasts

Your Teen with Sue and Steph

Focused on equipping parents with practical advice for the teen years, this podcast addresses many challenges and offers solutions. Hosts Sue and Steph guide listeners through adolescence with wisdom and humor. podcasts.apple.com/us/podcast/your-teen-with-sue-and-steph/id742654046

The podcasts highlighted span an extensive spectrum, addressing the multifaceted experiences of parenting teens; from deciphering the intricacies of their evolving minds to steering through societal expectations and educational hurdles. Through expert counsel, hands-on strategies, and authentic narratives, their goal is to enhance your resources and reduce the sense of seclusion that can frequently be a part of guiding teens toward adulthood.

While these podcasts can become part of the toolkit and are invaluable resources, it's crucial to acknowledge the distinctiveness of every teen's life. Expert opinions and communal narratives provide a compass, yet the essence of your teen's experience is rooted in the heartfelt dialogue, empathy, and bond you share. The course you chart with your son—marked by triumphs, setbacks, joyous moments, and lessons—will always be profoundly personal.

Organizations

Raising and mentoring teen boys often necessitates the support of broader communities and dedicated organizations. These institutions, with their rich history and specialized focus areas—ranging from mental well-being and community engagement to skill development and outdoor adventures—have provided invaluable guidance to numerous families. Through their comprehensive resources, programs, and mentorship opportunities, they not only address potential challenges but also forge nurturing environments where teen boys can thrive and achieve their fullest potential.

Big Brothers Big Sisters of America pairs youth with volunteer mentors to guide and support them, instilling confidence, fostering academic excellence, and helping them avoid detrimental behaviors. This organization's mentoring relationships are known to create lasting positive impacts on mentors and mentees. www.bbbs.org

One of the US's premier youth organizations, the **Boy Scouts of America (BSA)**, employs outdoor-centric activities like camping, aquatic events, and hiking to instill values of responsibility, service, and leadership in young participants. Through hands-on experiences, members learn essential life skills. www.scouting.org

Dedicated to serving children, youth, and families, the **Boys & Girls Aid Society** offers many services ranging from foster care and adoption to counseling. The organization's primary goal is to ensure every child grows up in a loving and stable environment. www.boysandgirlsaid.org

Boys & Girls Clubs of America is a haven for young individuals, providing a safe environment to learn, play, and develop. Their multifaceted programs encompass education, arts, sports, and character development, creating well-rounded individuals. www.bgca.org

Boys To Men Mentoring Network provides teen boys with a supportive community of men who offer encouragement, share their struggles, and empower the youth. Their approach ensures consistent support, celebrates the boys' strengths, and helps them navigate challenges. www.boystomen.org

A worldwide Christian youth organization, **Boy's Brigade** blends drills, skill enhancement, and faith. Their modules emphasize personal growth, community service, and comprehensive development, helping young boys become responsible community members. Boys-brigade.org.uk

Child Mind Institute serves children and families grappling with mental health and learning disorders. Their tailored resources and support services create transformative changes in the lives of young individuals, especially teen boys. www.childmind.org

JED Foundation centers on safeguarding the emotional well-being of teenagers and young adults. With resources, collaborative efforts, and strong advocacy, they are proactive in areas of mental health and suicide prevention. www.jedfoundation.org

A premier national mentoring initiative, **Mentoring USA** collaborates with other entities to furnish mentors for youth in need. Their comprehensive mentoring strategies bolster youth in academic, personal, and passion-driven areas. www.mentoringusa.org

The National Alliance on Mental Illness (NAMI) is a linchpin in mental health advocacy, striving to enhance the lives of those touched by mental illnesses. Their youth-centric support groups, educational modules, and resources are pivotal for teens and their families. www.nami.org

National Youth Alliance for Boys and Men of Color is an amalgamation of five youth-organizing networks that zealously work toward elevating the leadership roles of young men of color. They are relentless in their mission to drive change in their communities. www. abmoc.org or www.fcyo.org

ReachOut USA is an informative and supportive hub for teens and young adults undergoing tough phases or mental health challenges. Their digital resources are designed to be accessible and relevant. ReachOut.com

Teen Line is a sanctuary where teens can converse with trained peers about their challenges. This organization ensures teenagers have a nonjudgmental platform to voice their concerns and procure advice. www.teenlineonline.org

A global institution, **YMCA**'s diverse programs like sports, swimming, and educational endeavors nurture the latent potential in children and teens. They also encourage healthy lifestyles and instill values of social responsibility. www.ymca.org

The multifaceted experiences of teen boys can be significantly enhanced by leveraging the extensive support these organizations provide. These entities not only represent a reservoir of resources and programs but are also emblematic of the broader community's dedication to championing the development, comprehension, and overall well-being of its younger generations. As you delve deeper into what these organizations offer, recognize that it's through such collective endeavors and partnerships that teen boys garner the affirmation, challenges, and experiences pivotal to their journey toward adulthood.

Support Groups

Among the many available resources, support groups stand out with their distinctive ability to cultivate profound human connections. These groups offer a sanctuary for parents, professionals, and teens alike, enabling them to exchange experiences, learn collaboratively, and find solace in the understanding that they're not alone. As individuals grapple with the complexities of raising and understanding teen boys, these support groups illuminate the path with authentic discussions, empathy, and collective support.

Al-Anon Family Groups

These support groups are specifically tailored for friends and families of individuals grappling with alcohol-related challenges. Parents can find solace, share personal experiences, and gain insights on helping their teen boys battling addiction. www.al-anon.org

American Foundation for Suicide Prevention (AFSP)

AFSP offers regional chapters running support groups for those affected by suicide. They host essential sessions for parents confronting the complex emotions and implications arising from a teen son's struggles with suicidal tendencies. www.afsp.org

Boys to Men Mentoring Network

This mentoring initiative assists boys aged 14–24 as they transition to manhood. Especially beneficial for those encountering personal challenges, teen boys can derive support, guidance, and mentorship through group interactions. www.boystomen.org

Education Week's Group for Teachers of Boys

This digital forum enables educators to exchange ideas, methods, and experiences about teaching and assisting male students. It's a pivotal resource for professionals who desire to enhance their methodologies when engaging with teen boys. You will find relevant discussions on *Education Week*'s main website. www.edweek.org

Facebook Groups for Parenting Teens

These digital communities offer parents a space to seek advice, share experiences, and receive support concerning teen-related challenges. From discipline to trust-building, these groups provide insights to navigate dilemmas like body image issues, dating, and more. They are available on Facebook's platform. You can search for them directly on Facebook.

Men's Health Network

While catering to all male age groups, this network provides vital resources and platforms for health discussions. It champions overall health, offering teen boys and men a space to address and discuss prevalent health issues. www.menshealthnetwork.org

National Parent Helpline

This dedicated helpline delivers emotional reinforcements to parents managing day-to-day challenges, ensuring they aren't navigating parenthood alone. Additionally, it connects them to valuable community resources tailored to their needs. www.nationalparenthelpline.org

Parents Helping Parents (PHP)

PHP is a national network delivering support groups for parents navigating the multifaceted challenges their children encounter, including academic hurdles and behavioral concerns. Parents of teen boys can discover a sense of community and shared understanding here. www.parentsanonymous.org

Teen Parent Connection

Specially designed for young parents, this group fosters a judgment-free zone where young moms and dads can share experiences and derive support from peers, ensuring they're not facing parenthood challenges alone. www.teenparentconnection.org

The Trevor Project

Catering primarily to LGBTQ+ youth, this organization provides crisis intervention and suicide prevention services. For teen boys within the

LGBTQ+ community, their support groups and helplines are pivotal in offering assistance and understanding. www.thetrevorproject.org

Young Men's Health (Boston Children's Hospital)

This platform delivers resources for teen boys to grasp and address their health concerns effectively. Additionally, it helps professionals comprehend and tackle health and developmental challenges associated with teen boys. www.youngmenshealthsite.org

The strength derived from shared experiences, collective wisdom, or a simple empathetic gesture within a group setting is profound. As you explore these support groups, recognize that they embody communities that consistently offer hope, guidance, and unity. Whether you aim to comprehend, assist, or just stand by a teen boy, these groups provide the cherished company of individuals who've "been there." Within these collective environments, answers surface, resilience is nurtured, and, above all, pathways to more profound understanding are established.

Books & Publications

Literature can provide insights, well-researched findings, and empathetic viewpoints on parenting, comprehending, and mentoring teen boys. Spanning topics from the scientific intricacies of the adolescent mind to the contemporary challenges posed by a digital-centric world, this curated collection of books serves as essential guides. They offer foundational understanding and pragmatic solutions for those eager to navigate the complexities of today's adolescent tribulations.

- *Blame My Brain: The Amazing Teenage Brain Revealed* by Nicola Morgan (2013): This book offers a humorous and relatable exploration of the intricacies of the teenage brain. Nicola Morgan touches upon topics like mood swings, sleep patterns, risk-taking behavior, gender differences, and the roots of addiction.

- *Brainstorm: The Power and Purpose of the Teenage Brain* by Daniel J. Siegel (2014): Dr. Siegel illuminates the intricate workings of the teenage brain from a neurobiological perspective. His advice helps parents transform adolescent challenges into golden opportunities for growth.

- *Boys Should Be Boys: 7 Secrets to Raising Healthy Sons* by Meg Meeker (2008): Dr. Meeker provides insightful and actionable advice on raising boys in today's complex society. She touches upon the values, habits, and characteristics that form the foundation for a well-rounded and resilient young man.

- *Building Resilience in Children and Teens: Giving Kids Roots and Wings* by Kenneth R. Ginsburg (2005): Focused on nurturing resilience, Dr. Ginsburg offers strategies that empower kids to handle life's challenges. Through his guidance, parents can help their children become self-reliant and confident adults.

- *Hooked on Games: The Lure and Cost of Video Game and Internet Addiction* by Andrew Doan and Brooke Strickland (2012): This book dives deep into the intricate world of gaming addiction, revealing its psychological and physical toll. Doan and Strickland offer valuable advice to those seeking equilibrium in the digital age.

- *iGen: Why Today's Super-connected Kids Are Growing Up Less Rebellious, More Tolerant, Less Happy—and Completely Unprepared for Adulthood—and What That Means for the Rest of Us* by Jean M. Twenge (2019): In this research-rich exploration, Dr. Twenge uncovers the unique dynamics of the iGeneration. Her insights equip parents, educators, and professionals with tools to support and understand this tech-savvy yet emotionally complex cohort.

- *I would, but my DAMN MIND won't let me!: A Teen's Guide to Controlling Their Thoughts and Feelings* (Words of Wisdom for Teens #2) by Jacqui Letran (2016): Jacqui Letran offers teens a hands-on guide to master their thoughts and emotions. This self-help book addresses the unique mental challenges faced by today's youth.

- *Masterminds and Wingmen: Helping Our Boys Cope with Schoolyard Power, Locker-Room Tests, Girlfriends, and the New Rules of Boy World* by Rosalind Wiseman (2013): With insights directly from teen boys, Wiseman reveals the pressures and complexities of their inner lives. The book addresses school challenges, intense emotions, and the digital era's unique struggles.

- *Parenting Teens with Love and Logic: Preparing Adolescents for Responsible Adulthood* by Foster Cline, MD & Jim Fay (2020): This book offers parents tools to foster responsibility and maturity in tweens and teens. Dr. Cline and Jim Fay provide strategies for setting boundaries, nurturing skills, and encouraging decision-making without resorting to anger or power plays.

- *Permission to Feel: Unlocking the Power of Emotions to Help Our Kids, Ourselves, and Our Society Thrive* by Marc Brackett (2019): As an authority on emotional intelligence, Brackett offers tools to label, comprehend, and manage emotions. His approach helps promote emotional growth and mental well-being in young people.

- *Raising Boys by Design: A Unique Blueprint for Encouraging Healthy Mental, Emotional, and Spiritual Development in Today's Boys* by Gregory L. Jantz and Michael Gurian: Jantz and Gurian combine neuroscience research and practical wisdom to offer a comprehensive guide for nurturing modern boys. Their insights help parents raise emotionally, mentally, and spiritually healthy sons.

- *Raising Cain: Protecting the Emotional Life of Boys* by Dan Kindlon (2013): This seminal work dives into the emotional life of boys, underscoring the importance of emotional intelligence and protection. Kindlon offers insights and strategies for parents and educators to understand and nurture the emotional lives of their sons.

- *Raising Resilient Children: Fostering Strength, Hope, and Optimism in Your Child* by Robert B. Brooks (2000): Dr. Brooks delves into the challenges and rewards of parenting teens. He provides insights and strategies for nurturing resilience and optimism in young individuals.

- *Slow Parenting Teens: How to Create a Positive, Respectful, and Fun Relationship with Your Teenager* by Molly Wingate, MA (2012): Molly Wingate presents solutions tailored for the modern challenges of parenting teenagers. Her approach emphasizes positivity, respect, and building meaningful connections.

- *The Grown-Up's Guide to Teenage Humans: How to Decode Their Behavior, Develop Trust, and Raise a Respectable Adult* by Josh Shipp (2017): Penned by a former "at-risk teen," the book serves as a guide for understanding, trusting, and raising teens into mature adults. Shipp shares the profound influence of a persistent foster father.

- *The Tech-Wise Family: Everyday Steps for Putting Technology in Its Proper Place* by Andy Crouch (2017): Crouch delves into the digital age's challenges, focusing on technology's impact on family dynamics. He provides actionable steps to establish tech boundaries, ensuring balance and addressing potential pitfalls like gaming addiction.

- *Uncommon Sense for Parents with Teenagers* by Michael Riera (2012): Riera offers practical and insightful advice for parents navigating the teenage years. His guidance fosters understanding, communication, and trust.

- *When Good Kids Do Bad Things: A Survival Guide for Parents of Teenagers* by Katherine Gordy Levine (2013): Levine crafts a survival guide for parents experiencing challenges with their teens. Her insights and strategies bridge misunderstandings and foster positive parent-teen relationships.

- *Why Gender Matters, Second Edition: What Parents and Teachers Need to Know about the Emerging Science of Sex Differences* by Leonard Sax (2017): In this updated edition, Dr. Sax delves into the science behind gender differences, discussing implications for raising and educating boys and girls. He addresses various topics, from digital distractions and academics to mental health.

In an era marked by swift shifts in technology, culture, and societal expectations, these handpicked books illuminate the way with scientific data, seasoned insights, and compassionate counsel. While each offers a distinct lens through which to view the world of teen boys, collectively, they impart knowledge that can empower our efforts to nurture their emotional, mental, and holistic development. While these resources offer guiding principles, the individual experience of every teen and parent will resonate uniquely, creating their own narratives inspired by the wisdom found within these pages.

Online Platforms and Apps

In a time of digital interconnectedness, a multitude of online platforms and applications stand out as potent resources tailored to diverse requirements. These platforms make invaluable resources accessible;

they contribute to enhancing academic proficiency, ensuring mental well-being, and promoting effective parenting. For parents and teens going through the complexities of adolescence, these digital tools provide unmatched guidance, assistance, and opportunities to forge supportive communities.

BetterHelp is an online counseling platform that connects individuals with licensed therapists for private web-based counseling sessions. BetterHelp offers an accessible way for teens and parents to seek professional mental health support. www.betterhelp.com

Brainly is a community-driven educational platform where students can ask questions and get answers from fellow students and educators. It provides a collaborative space for academic learning and problem-solving, assisting teens in grasping complex topics. www.brainly.com

A leading app for meditation and sleep, **Calm** offers guided meditations, sleep stories, breathing exercises, and relaxing music. Designed to foster emotional well-being and reduce stress, it's an excellent tool for teens needing a relaxation break. www.calm.com

Designed with safety in mind, **Circle of 6** lets users quickly contact six trusted friends when they feel unsafe or at risk. This app equips teens with a convenient way to reach out, ensuring their safety and security. www.circleof6app.com

Cozi Family Organizer helps families manage their busy lives by offering features like shared calendars and to-do lists. This app is helpful for parents and teens juggling multiple schedules and tasks. www.cozi.com

Coursera offers courses from top universities and institutions on various subjects. Ideal for teens and young adults, the online learning

platform promotes academic excellence and skill acquisition. www.
coursera.org

An interactive language-learning app, **Duolingo** offers lessons in
multiple languages. Engaging lessons help teens expand their linguistic
capabilities and understand different cultures. www.duolingo.com

FamilyTime allows parents to monitor their child's smartphone
activities. This tool ensures safety and appropriate use for teens and
younger children. www.familytime.io

FindMyKids is a GPS tracker app that offers live location tracking,
among other features. Tailored for families, it's suitable for tracking
teenagers, ensuring safety for the kids and peace of mind for the
parents. www.findmykids.org

Headspace provides guided meditations, mindfulness exercises, and
sleep aids. Its user-friendly interface promotes mental well-being and
encourages users, including teens, to incorporate meditation into their
daily routines. www.headspace.com

A nonprofit educational entity, **Khan Academy** delivers free online
lessons on numerous subjects, from math to humanities. With
comprehensive resources, it fosters independent learning and
academic achievement for teens. www.khanacademy.org

An all-in-one parental control app, **Kids360** offers tools for
monitoring and managing a child's digital activities. It helps parents
ensure their teen's safety and appropriate internet use. www.
kids360now.com

Mighty Networks facilitates the creation and joining of niche
communities based on interests or challenges. This platform is a

dynamic space where parents and teens can connect with like-minded individuals and share valuable experiences. www.mightynetworks.com

A digital monitoring tool, **Net Nanny** assists parents in overseeing their child's online habits. By providing insights into digital activities, it ensures safe and responsible internet use by teens. www. netnanny.com

Using parental control tools and family locator functionalities, **OurPact** is designed for modern families. Parents can set digital boundaries and track their teen's location for safety. www.ourpact.com

Focused on educational gaming, **PBS Parents Play and Learn** provides a collection of interactive activities for children. While it's incredibly engaging for younger kids, it can also serve as a resource for older children looking for educational games. pbskids.org/apps/pbs-parents-play--learn.html

A multifunctional parental control app, **Qustodio** offers monitoring tools and well-being features. It helps parents enforce balanced digital habits and emphasize emotional well-being for their teens. www. qustodio.com

A comprehensive online therapy platform, **Talkspace** connects users with licensed therapists through various mediums. By offering consistent mental health support, it's a boon for teens and parents alike. www.talkspace.com

Teachable is an online platform that empowers experts to create and sell courses. It allows teens to explore fresh skills or deepen their knowledge in particular areas. www.teachable.com

As we increasingly integrate technology into our daily routines, the power of these online platforms and apps becomes evident. These resources can be lifelines, offering tailored solutions and community connections that were once beyond reach; they guide teens and parents toward growth, understanding, and mutual support. While the tools listed here offer vast benefits, users must approach them with discernment, ensuring each platform aligns with individual goals and values.

Workshops & Seminars

As society grapples with the complexities of raising and guiding teen boys in modern times, workshops and seminars have emerged as pivotal avenues for direct learning and engagement. These events, facilitated by seasoned professionals and experts, offer targeted insights and hands-on strategies to address the nuanced challenges of adolescence. They provide evidence-based solutions and foster community, enabling participants to share experiences and learn from one another.

Challenger Seminars: Engaging the Disengaged Teen

Designed to tackle the challenges of motivating disengaged teens, this seminar provides comprehensive strategies to parents, educators, and professionals. By understanding the root causes of disengagement, participants are equipped with actionable solutions to reignite passion and drive in teenage boys. www.teenagewhisperer.co.uk

Common Sense Parenting: Navigating the Teen Years

This workshop is crafted for parents to gain a deeper understanding of the tumultuous teen years. It offers invaluable strategies for effective communication, establishing boundaries, and fostering a trusting, positive relationship with teenage boys. teenhealthconnection.org/parenting-programs

Gaming Addictions: Understanding and Overcoming

This in-depth seminar probes into the realm of gaming addiction, dissecting its impact on mental well-being. Parents and teens are provided with actionable strategies to strike a healthy balance between gaming leisure and other essential life responsibilities. gamequitters.com

Parenting Programs | BGC Canada

These workshops are designed to help parents fortify their family strengths. Through the sessions, participants learn about adolescent brain development and gain practical strategies for effectively parenting a preteen or teenager. www.futureswithoutviolence.org/the-amazing-teen-brain-what-every-parent-needs-to-know

Raising Boys—Maggie Dent

Maggie Dent's seminar series encompasses multiple webinars and masterclasses on raising boys. Topics range from nurturing younger boys ("Dear Little Boys" and "Mothering Our Boys") to addressing the challenges of tween and teen years ("From Boys to Men" series) and the comprehensive journey from babyhood to adulthood. www.maggiedent.com/common-concerns/raising-boys

Workshops and seminars are invaluable resources that encompass a breadth of topics, from the intricacies of the adolescent brain to the nuances of modern social pressures and academic hurdles. These sessions offer practical advice, expert insights, and relatable narratives to parents, educators, and guardians; they are designed to arm attendees with knowledge and tools, making parenting feel less solitary and more navigable. They foster an environment of shared experiences, facilitating peer engagement and collective growth. As the dynamics of parenting and mentoring evolve, staying abreast through such avenues ensures we remain adept, compassionate, and effective in our interactions with teens. Embracing these learning opportunities is our gateway to being more informed, connected, and confident in our roles.

Digital Awareness and Safety

In today's digital age, navigating the online world safely and responsibly has become paramount for everyone, especially our younger generation. As teens become increasingly active online, the potential threats they might encounter—from cyberbullying to privacy breaches—have become a significant concern for parents, educators, and communities. This Digital Awareness and Safety resources section provides a robust framework and tools to ensure that every online interaction is knowledgeable and secure. With these resources at your fingertips, you can confidently guide the young internet users in your life to make informed and safe digital choices.

Google's initiative, **Be Internet Awesome**, educates kids on digital citizenship and safety. It comprises lessons on vital topics such as phishing, safeguarding personal details, and discerning trustworthy sources online. beinternetawesome.withgoogle.com/en_us

Common Sense Media is a comprehensive guide for parents, offering reviews and ratings of various media, from movies to apps. Parents learn to decipher the content their children might encounter online and get valuable advice on setting tech boundaries within the family. www.commonsensemedia.org

The **Cyberbullying Research Center** is a hub of resources dedicated to understanding, preventing, and addressing cyberbullying. It provides actionable prevention strategies, delves into the legal nuances of online harassment, and offers tools to effectively combat cyberbullying. cyberbullying.org

Digital Citizenship Institute fosters digital citizenship by encouraging collaboration, community engagement, and responsible online behavior. Through its resources, it emphasizes respect, empathy, and proactive actions in the virtual world. www.zoominfo. com/c/digital-citizenship-institute/459145426

An extension of Google's Be Internet Awesome initiative, **Digital Safety Resources—Be Internet Awesome** further supports families in understanding and practicing online safety. It offers tools and guidance, making the incorporation of safe digital habits seamless and practical in daily life. beinternetawesome.withgoogle.com/en_us/families

An international nonprofit, the **Family Online Safety Institute (FOSI)** dedicates itself to enhancing the digital well-being of families. It offers many tools, resources, and events, all tailored to promote online safety and responsible tech use. www.fosi.org

Internet Matters is a not-for-profit entity that guides families on the intricacies of the digital age. From setting up controls on devices to comprehending the latest digital trends and mitigating online risks, it's a comprehensive guide for parents. www.internetmatters.org

NetSmartz (National Center for Missing & Exploited Children) provides a diverse range of resources tailored for various age groups to understand and mitigate online risks. From kids to law enforcement officials, it offers insights into online dangers and strategies to counter them effectively. www.missingkids.org/netsmartz/home

Online Safety for Youth—The Office of Justice Programs compiles a range of materials and websites, both federal and federally supported, that focus on the online safety of youth. It serves as a guide for parents, educators, and caregivers, offering insights into the online risks children face and the safe strategies to employ. www.ojp.gov/feature/internet-safety/online-safety-youth

Raising Digital Citizens—National Cybersecurity Alliance is a comprehensive resource that covers various facets of online behavior, from cyberbullying and sexting to social networking. Additionally, it features the FBI's Safe Online Surfing (SOS) Internet Challenge, which educates students on online security essentials. staysafeonline.org/online-safety-privacy-basics/raising-digital-citizens

Held annually, **Safer Internet Day** champions the responsible and positive use of digital technology, with a focus on children and young individuals. The event comprises discussions, resources, and strategies to foster a safer online community for the younger generation.

StaySafeOnline, backed by the National Cyber Security Alliance, offers extensive resources to ensure a secure online experience for users. It accentuates the importance of cybersecurity, privacy, and general online safety, equipping users with knowledge for safer digital navigation. staysafeonline.org

UK Safer Internet Centre ensures children and young individuals can navigate the internet securely. It offers a wide range of e-safety tips, expert advice, and resources, making the internet a safer place for younger users. saferinternet.org.uk

These resources provide valuable information on navigating the
digital world safely and responsibly. They offer practical advice, expert
insights, and real-life stories that can help teens make informed and
safe digital choices. Digital safety is not just about setting restrictions
but about fostering an environment where young users can understand,
evaluate, and make informed decisions in the digital landscape. By
utilizing the resources provided in this section, parents, educators, and
teens themselves can become well-equipped to face the ever-evolving
challenges of the online world. As the digital realm continues to grow
and shape our lives, let's ensure that safety, respect, and responsibility
become its foundational pillars. We urge you to explore these resources,
share them with others, and, most importantly, engage in continuous
conversations about digital well-being.

Expert Directory

As you work on understanding and guiding teen boys, turning to
experts who have dedicated their careers to researching, analyzing,
and offering solutions becomes invaluable. The individuals listed in
this directory are not just names but pillars in adolescent psychology
and counseling. Their collective wisdom, derived from years of
professional experience and scholarly work, shines a light on the
nuanced challenges and triumphs of teen boyhood.

- **Dr. Carl Pickhardt** A psychologist emphasizing the
  intricacies of adolescence, Dr. Pickhardt has penned multiple
  insightful books on the topic. His work, *Surviving Your
  Child's Adolescence: How to Understand, and Even Enjoy, the
  Rocky Road to Independence* (2013), offers parents valuable
  perspectives and advice.

- **Dr. Dan Kindlon** A distinguished clinical and research
  psychologist, Dr. Kindlon specializes in understanding

behavioral challenges in children and adolescents. Among his renowned publications is *Raising Cain: Protecting the Emotional Life of Boys* (2000), which sheds light on the emotional facets of boyhood.

- **Dr. Daniel J. Siegel** Affiliated with the UCLA School of Medicine, Dr. Siegel is a recognized authority on topics like the teenage brain, mindfulness, and interpersonal neurobiology. His expertise bridges the gap between clinical practice and holistic approaches to adolescent well-being.

- **Dr. Frances E. Jensen** With a rich background in neurology, especially pediatric neurology, Dr. Jensen investigates the nuances of brain development. Her book, *The Teenage Brain: A Neuroscientist's Survival Guide to Raising Adolescents and Young Adults* (2016), offers parents and educators deep insights into adolescent brain processes.

- **Dr. Harold S. Koplewicz** A vanguard in child and adolescent psychiatry, Dr. Koplewicz founded the Child Mind Institute, championing mental health causes for kids. His dedication and expertise have established him as a central figure in child and adolescent mental well-being.

- **Dr. Ken Ginsburg** Based at the Children's Hospital of Philadelphia, Dr. Ginsburg's expertise lies in adolescent medicine, emphasizing resilience. He is particularly interested in understanding and empowering teenagers, especially those facing adversity and challenges.

- **Dr. Laurence Steinberg** An eminent voice in understanding adolescence, Dr. Steinberg has authored several seminal works on the subject. His book *Age of Opportunity: Lessons from the New Science of Adolescence* (2015) is particularly noteworthy for its deep dive into adolescent development.

- **Dr. Leonard Sax** Known for *Boys Adrift* (2016), Dr. Sax investigates the factors influencing boys and young men today.

As a family physician and psychologist, he presents a unique lens on gender differences and developmental stages.

- **Dr. Michael Gurian** In *The Wonder of Boys* (2006), Dr. Gurian blends neurobiology with sociocultural perspectives, offering a comprehensive view of boyhood. His work helps parents, educators, and professionals understand and guide boys' development.

- **Dr. Michael Thompson** Dr. Thompson, a respected psychologist and author, delves into the emotional and social challenges that boys grapple with. His contributions help demystify the often-misunderstood inner worlds of boys.

- **Dr. Roni Cohen-Sandler** Dr. Cohen-Sandler's expertise centers around the dynamics of parent-teen relationships and adolescent well-being. By focusing on the concerns of teenagers and their families, she offers valuable strategies and insights to foster healthier dynamics.

- **Dr. William Pollack** Operating from Harvard Medical School, Dr. Pollack's research centers on the emotional intricacies of boys and the societal perceptions of masculinity. His book *Real Boys* (1999) provides a compelling critique of conventional boyhood myths and highlights the challenges boys face.

These experts have made significant contributions to our understanding of adolescent psychology and have provided valuable insights for parents, educators, and professionals working with teenagers. The depth and breadth of knowledge of these experts serve as a foundation for parents, educators, and caregivers. By diving into their research, attending their talks, or seeking their counsel, one can gain a more comprehensive grasp of the issues at hand and the best approaches to address them. As the landscape of teen challenges evolves, staying connected with such thought leaders ensures we remain informed, prepared, and proactive in our roles as guides and mentors.

Physical Health Resources

In the era of digital connectivity, physical health often takes a back seat. Yet, a strong foundation of physical well-being is crucial, not just for our bodies but for our minds and spirits as well. For the younger generation, establishing a pattern of healthy living early on can set the stage for a lifetime of benefits. The resources listed in this section cater to diverse physical health needs, including understanding the intricacies of nutrition, finding an engaging sports program, or addressing body image concerns, and these reputable organizations provide valuable guidance and support.

American College of Sports Medicine (ACSM) is a leading authority in sports medicine and exercise science. They provide comprehensive guidelines and valuable resources tailored to promote physical activity across different age groups. www.acsm.org/certification

The Boys & Girls Clubs of America offers specialized programs designed to encourage physical fitness, reduce stress, and instill teamwork values among the youth in their programs. These initiatives foster a sense of camaraderie and well-being among participants. www.bgca.org/programs/sports-recreation

Centers for Disease Control and Prevention (CDC) provides evidence-based guidelines and resources tailored for individuals spanning all age groups. They promote regular physical activity, leading to enhanced overall health and well-being. ww.cdc.gov/physicalactivity/resources/recommendations.html

Eatright.org (Academy of Nutrition and Dietetics) is a platform that offers nutritional guidelines emphasizing healthy eating habits.

It provides many resources that focus on proper diet and nutrition suitable for all age groups. www.eatright.org

KidsHealth from Nemours offers a comprehensive look into the health aspects pertinent to children and teenagers. Their guidance spans nutrition, exercise, body image, and more, ensuring a holistic approach to youth health. kidshealth.org

Let's Move! is an initiative geared toward battling childhood obesity. It accentuates the importance of healthier food choices and increased physical activity for children and teenagers. letsmove. obamawhitehouse.archives.gov

McMillen Health sheds light on the concept of physical health and the myriad factors influencing it. Their insights enhance understanding and promote a more holistic approach to well-being. www. mcmillenhealth.org

The **National Eating Disorders Association (NEDA)** stands as a vital resource providing tools, helplines, and information to address eating disorders and associated body image issues. Their resources are designed to help individuals understand and navigate these challenges. www.nationaleatingdisorders.org

The **National Institutes of Health (NIH)** offers a thorough guide to upholding physical health. This Physical Wellness Toolkit includes actionable tips on staying active, muscle maintenance, achieving a healthy weight, and cultivating beneficial habits. www.nih.gov/health-information/physical-wellness-toolkit

The **President's Council on Sports, Fitness & Nutrition** offers a range of resources and initiatives with a focus on health and wellness.

Their materials emphasize the importance of physical activity and balanced nutrition for individuals of all age brackets. health.gov/pcsfn

The **YMCA**'s Healthy Living Programs cater to various aspects of physical health. From exercise classes to nutritional counseling, their offerings are designed to befit all age demographics. www.ymca.org/what-we-do/healthy-living

Physical health is an intricate blend of regular exercise, balanced nutrition, mental wellness, and a positive self-image. By integrating the recommendations and guidelines from these trusted resources, individuals can craft a holistic approach to their health. Parents, educators, and mentors are pivotal in directing young people toward these resources.

Work and Career Guidance

The **American Association for Employment in Education (AAEE)** is a pivotal resource for aspiring and practicing educators in their job search, providing tools and opportunities. They offer networking events, career advice, and job search instruments tailored for educators. aaee.org

Big Interview offers expert training and unlimited interview practice through a subscription model. Job seekers can benefit from AI-based feedback to hone their interview skills. www.biginterview.com

The Bureau of Labor Statistics (BLS) delivers in-depth data on careers, industries, and employment trends. Their platform provides analytical insights into the evolving job market. www.bls.gov

CareerAddict stands as a comprehensive career resource website. It boasts expert insights and advice from professionals across diverse industries. www.careeraddict.com

CareerBuilder is a renowned job search platform that facilitates job hunting with various tools. Users can access job listings, salary comparisons, resume-building tools, and career advice. www. careerbuilder.com

CareerOneStop (Sponsored by the US Department of Labor) offers many tools for career exploration, training, and job seeking. Sponsored by the US Department of Labor, it's a holistic platform for job seekers. www.betterteam.com/careeronestop

Glassdoor gives job seekers a window into potential employers, detailing company cultures and salaries. Their platform also features reviews to help candidates make informed employment decisions. www.glassdoor.com/index.htm

Indeed ranks among the largest job search engines worldwide. It furnishes users with job listings, company reviews, salary data, and tools for resume crafting. www.indeed.com

LinkedIn Learning curates courses designed for skill enhancement and career advancement. Additionally, it doubles as a platform for professional networking and job hunting. learning.linkedin.com

Monster is a global job search engine that streamlines the job hunt with various services. It offers job listings, career advice, industry insights, and resume assistance. learning.linkedin.com

targetjobs centralizes information about career opportunities, primarily focusing on the UK's top graduate employers. The platform assists users in researching and applying for jobs and internships through employer profiles and advice. targetjobs.co.uk

Vault provides job seekers with company rankings, ratings, reviews, and more. It also offers blogs, forums, and career advice to guide users' career decisions. legacy.vault.com

Work It Daily delivers features like one-on-one coaching, resume reviews, and networking opportunities. They also provide tailored subscription packages for professionals at various career stages, from entry to executive levels. www.workitdaily.com

Each resource offers a unique perspective and toolset for individuals seeking guidance, information, and opportunities in their work and career paths. The myriad career opportunities available today are vast and varied. But with the proper guidance, finding a path that aligns with your skills, passions, and aspirations becomes less of a challenge. These resources offer a holistic approach to career development, from understanding job market trends to honing individual skills and connecting with potential employers.

Financial Education

In today's rapidly evolving world, teenagers are bombarded with many choices and challenges, many of which are influenced or amplified by financial considerations. From the allure of impulse buys in a digital marketplace to navigating student loans for higher education, the terrain of personal finance has become complex and, at times, treacherous. Yet, many of our educational systems lag in providing comprehensive financial education, leaving teens ill-equipped to navigate these waters. This section seeks to bridge that gap. Aimed at empowering our youth with the financial knowledge and confidence they need, we delve into money management, savings, credit, and even the psychological aspects of financial decision-making. By laying a solid foundation now, we aim to shape a generation of financially literate adults capable of making informed and sound financial decisions throughout their lives.

360 Degrees of Financial Literacy is an initiative by the American Institute of CPAs that offers tailored financial education resources for various life stages, including specialized content for teens. It enhances financial understanding through all phases of life. www.360financialliteracy.org

CashCourse delivers complimentary financial education resources for college students to equip them with practical financial management skills. The platform prepares students for real-life financial decisions. www.cashcourse.org

The **Consumer Financial Protection Bureau (CFPB)** offers an extensive collection of financial education materials, such as guides, worksheets, and posters, with many available in multiple languages. These resources can be downloaded or ordered in bulk to assist in financial learning. www.consumerfinance.gov

EverFi provides teens with an interactive, game-based financial curriculum, teaching essential financial skills through engaging real-life scenarios. This platform makes learning about finance both educational and entertaining. everfi.com/k-12/financial-education

The **FDIC (Federal Deposit Insurance Corporation)** offers Money Smart for Young People, a series of age-appropriate financial curriculums to help young individuals, from preschoolers to twenty-year-olds, develop financial literacy. These resources make financial concepts accessible and understandable for youth. www.fdic.gov/

resources/consumers/money-smart/teach-money-smart/money-smart-for-young-people/index.html

The **FDIC** also provides resources designed to facilitate collaboration between banks and schools to enhance the financial skills and experiences of young people. The Youth Banking Resource Center seeks to integrate practical financial education into school curriculums. www.fdic.gov/resources/consumers/youth-banking-resource-center/index.html

Fidelity includes a section on their website devoted to educating teens about finances, featuring articles on investment basics and credit building. The resources help teens develop sound financial habits early on. www.fidelity.com

Jump$tart Coalition is dedicated to advancing financial literacy among students by offering a range of educational resources, initiatives, and events. Their efforts are focused on providing practical financial knowledge to students. www.jumpstart.org

Money Prodigy delivers a selection of complimentary financial literacy activities for high schools, covering budgeting and money management. These activities help students understand and navigate various financial subjects. www.moneyprodigy.com

As the US government's official website for financial education, **MyMoney.gov** offers an array of tools and resources to teach the essentials of financial literacy to young adults and youths. The site serves as a comprehensive guide for basic financial knowledge. www.mymoney.gov

The **National Endowment for Financial Education (NEFE)** offers the High School Financial Planning Program, which delivers a structured financial literacy curriculum for high school students, emphasizing foundational personal finance skills. This program imparts essential financial knowledge relevant to teenagers. High School Financial Planning Program | HSFPP | NEFE

Visa's Practical Money Skills provides various resources, such as games and lesson plans, to assist teens and educators in learning about personal finance management. It's a resource that enhances financial understanding through practical education. www. practicalmoneyskills.com/en

Smart About Money offers a variety of free courses and tools to support teens in making savvy financial choices regarding saving, spending, and borrowing. This resource focuses on helping teens navigate the financial aspects of their lives with confidence. www.fdic. gov/resources/consumers/money-smart/index.html

Teens Guide to Money presents a comprehensive online platform to help teens grasp finance essentials, covering savings, investing, and credit. The site demystifies financial concepts for a teen audience. www.moneygeek.com/financial-planning/personal-finance-for-teens

The tools and knowledge imparted in this section are foundational and meant to be built upon as one progresses through various life stages and faces new financial challenges and opportunities. The true value of this section lies not just in its content but in its application. We urge every teen stepping into personal finance and every adult guiding a young one to regularly revisit these principles, stay updated with the changing financial landscape, and continuously seek further knowledge.

Conclusion

As you work on understanding, supporting, and nurturing the teen boys in your life, every piece of information, every resource, and every shared experience is a step forward. We hope this Resource Guide helps address the multifaceted challenges that our young men face today. However, the landscape of teenage challenges and solutions is ever evolving. Staying informed, engaged, and proactive is essential.

The true essence of *Rescuing Our Sons* and this accompanying Resource Guide is not just about problem-solving. It's about creating a more empathetic, understanding, and inclusive environment for our teen boys to thrive in. It's about acknowledging their struggles and strengths, listening to their stories, and empowering them to navigate the complexities of growing up in today's world.

As you continue in your endeavors as a parent, educator, mentor, or friend, always value the immense power of consistent support, open communication, and unconditional love. These are the anchors that can help our teen boys weather any storm.

Thank you for your commitment to making a difference in the lives of our young men. Together, we can craft a brighter, more hopeful future for our sons, ensuring they grow into resilient, compassionate, and fulfilled adults.

Acknowledgments

I first need to acknowledge the strikingly efficient, affirming, challenging, and capable team at Mango Publishing. Specifically, I need to express particular thanks to Brenda Knight, Chris McKenney, A-L Noble, and Krishna Bhat. Know that my gratitude runs deep, and I am so very fortunate for the expertise and passion you bring to this work. This book is infinitely better with your assistance and guidance.

Along the way, friends and colleagues have encouraged me and loaned me crucial ideas and direction on a manuscript that sometimes seemed untenable and maddening. So, my endless thanks to Chad, Tiffany, Grace and Everett Owen; Heidi, June and Will Stevens; Todd, Cathy, Shayne and Jacey Adams; Ilene, Mark, Max and Charlotte Collins; Father John Cusick; Michael Hainey; Andrew Santella; Michelle Icard; Kyle Peters; Jack Darrow; Alex Van Dyke; Logan Kehle; Zachary Folkening and Bela Ghandi for your unwavering support.

I need to recognize my family, Julie, George and Lauren, for their input and their patience, along with serving as an often-unwitting audience to my frequent ramblings on this topic.

And finally, my gratitude goes out to all of the boys and young men I've worked with who have bravely shared with me their difficult stories, in session and out. You are all an important part of positive movement for your own generation of boys, girls, young men and young women. And your words and wisdom are certain to inspire future generations as well. Thank you all.

About the Author

Dr. John Duffy is a Chicago-based clinical psychologist, bestselling author, keynote speaker, and national media expert. He has helped clients through his private practice for twenty-five years, specializing in work with adolescents, young adults, and their parents. He has consistently provided the tools young people need to thrive through his empathy, knowledge, experience, and practice, and has written three books intended to provide parents with the tools to help their teens and young adults thrive in this persistent age of anxiety, including *Parenting the New Teen in the Age of Anxiety* and the bestselling *The Available Parent*. In addition, for more than a decade, Dr. Duffy has spoken to thousands of parents internationally through Fortune 500 corporate programs as well as PTAs and other parenting networks.

Dr. Duffy has written and contributed to articles for CNN, the *Washington Post*, *The New York Times*, *Your Teen*, and countless other media outlets. On television, he has been a regular contributing expert on *NewsNation* and *The Steve Harvey Show* and has shared his expertise in frequent appearances on CNN, the *Today Show*, and *Morning Blend*, as well as hundreds of appearances on local outlets. On radio, Dr. Duffy is a regularly appearing expert on *WGN, WLS*, and *NPR*. He has appeared as an expert guest on countless podcasts and has been the host of two popular podcasts himself.

Mango Publishing, established in 2014, publishes an eclectic list of books by diverse authors—both new and established voices—on topics ranging from business, personal growth, women's empowerment, LGBTQ studies, health, and spirituality to history, popular culture, time management, decluttering, lifestyle, mental wellness, aging, and sustainable living. We were named 2019 *and* 2020's #1 fastest growing independent publisher by *Publishers Weekly*. Our success is driven by our main goal, which is to publish high-quality books that will entertain readers as well as make a positive difference in their lives.

Our readers are our most important resource; we value your input, suggestions, and ideas. We'd love to hear from you—after all, we are publishing books for you!

Please stay in touch with us and follow us at:

Facebook: Mango Publishing
Twitter: @MangoPublishing
Instagram: @MangoPublishing
LinkedIn: Mango Publishing
Pinterest: Mango Publishing
Newsletter: mangopublishinggroup.com/newsletter

Join us on Mango's journey to reinvent publishing, one book at a time.

Printed in the USA
CPSIA information can be obtained
at www.ICGtesting.com
JSHW030854091123
51776JS00004B/4

9 781684 813681